FIRST 50
POP SONGS

YOU SHOULD PLAY ON DRUMS

ISBN 978-1-7051-6914-8

HAL•LEONARD®

Visit Hal Leonard Online at
www.halleonard.com

World headquarters, contact:
Hal Leonard
7777 West Bluemound Road
Milwaukee, WI 53213
Email: info@halleonard.com

In Europe, contact:
Hal Leonard Europe Limited
1 Red Place
London, W1K 6PL
Email: info@halleonardeurope.com

In Australia, contact:
Hal Leonard Australia Pty. Ltd.
4 Lentara Court
Cheltenham, Victoria, 3192 Australia
Email: info@halleonard.com.au

CONTENTS

Addicted to Love

Words and Music by Robert Palmer

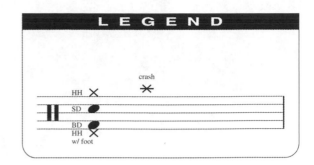

Intro
Moderately ♩ = 112

Play 3 times

Verse
The lights are   on,   but you're not   home...

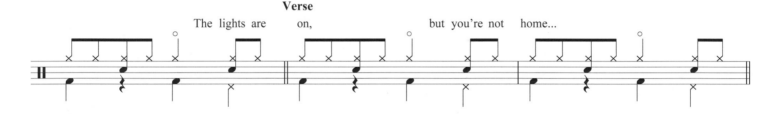

Verse
You can't   sleep,   you can't   eat...

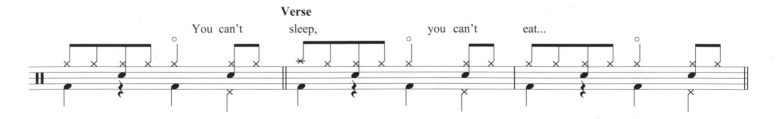

Chorus

as well face it, you're ad - dict - ed to love...

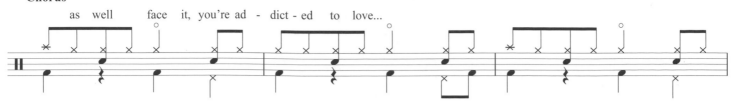

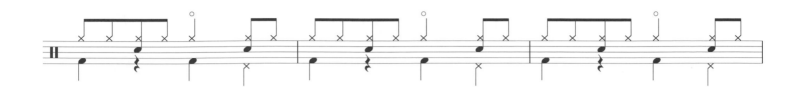

To Coda ⊕

Might as well face it, you're ad -

Guitar Solo

dict - ed to love.

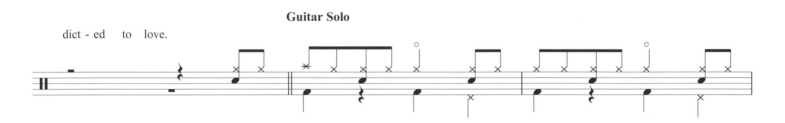

D.S. al Coda
(take repeats)

The lights are...

⊕ **Coda**

Begin fade

Fade out

Play 7 times

All Star

Words and Music by Greg Camp

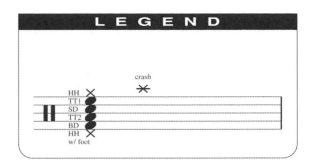

Verse

Moderately ♩ = 104

Well, the

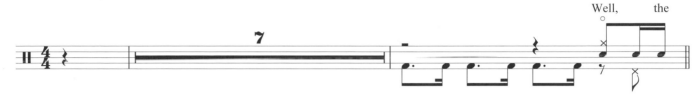

Verse

years start com-in', and they don't stop com-in'...

Chorus

Hey now,   you're an all star...

1.   2.

It's a

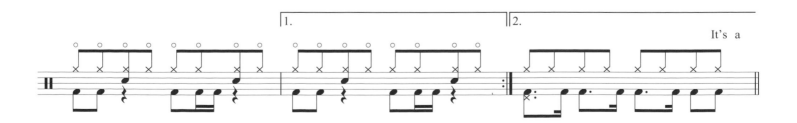

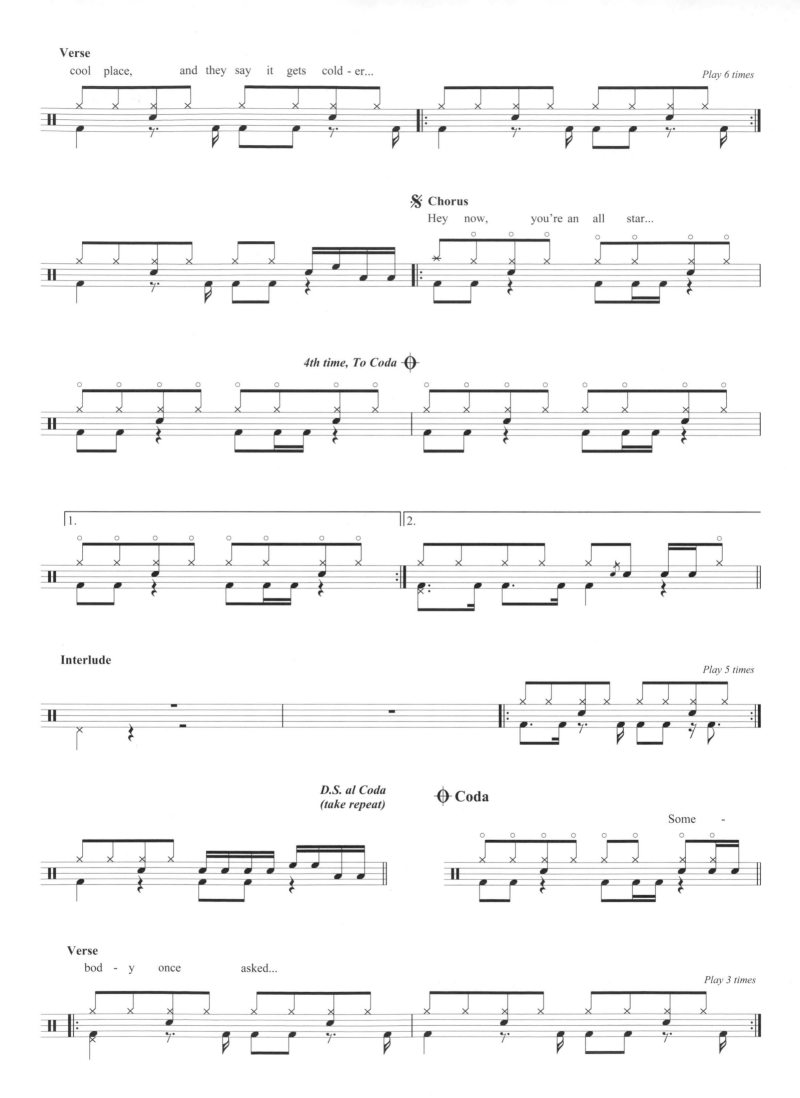

Well,   the

Verse

years   start   com-in',   and   they   don't   stop   com-in'...

Play 6 times

Chorus

Hey   now,   you're   an   all   star...

1.

2.

Billie Jean

Words and Music by Michael Jackson

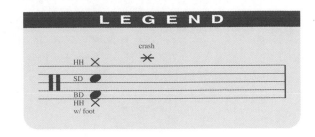

Intro
Moderate Pop ♩ = 117

Verse

She was more like a beau-

Play 7 times

ty queen...

Play 9 times

Pre-Chorus

Peo-ple al - ways told me, be care-ful of what you do...

Play 3 times

Chorus

Bil - lie Jean is not my lov - er...

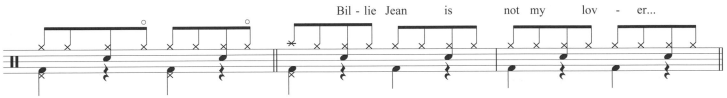

Play 4 times

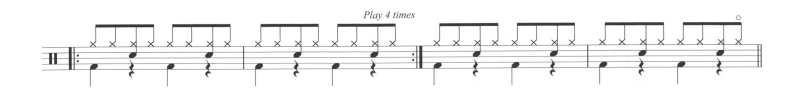

Verse

For for-ty days and for for-ty nights...

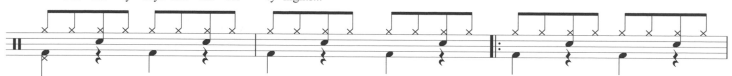

She told my ba-by we danced till three...

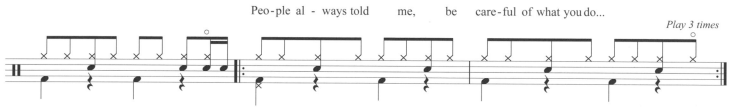

Pre-Chorus

Peo-ple al-ways told me, be care-ful of what you do...

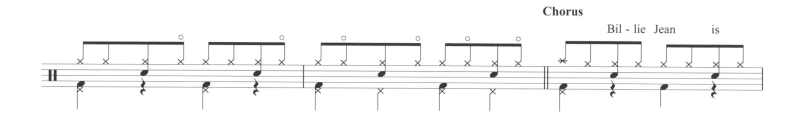

Chorus

Bil-lie Jean is

not my lov - er...

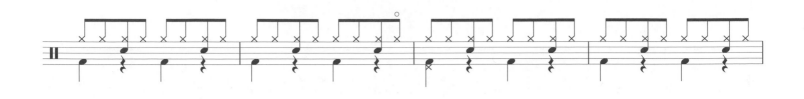

Interlude

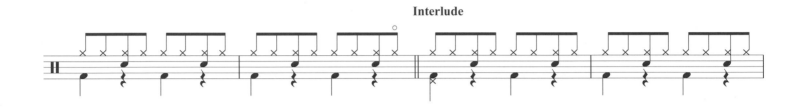

She says I   am the one...

Chorus

Bil - lie Jean   is

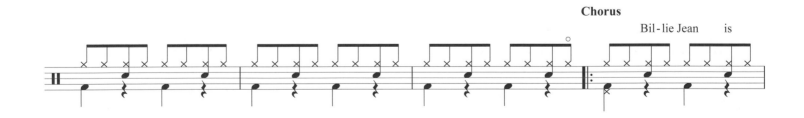

not my   lov - er...   *Repeat and fade*

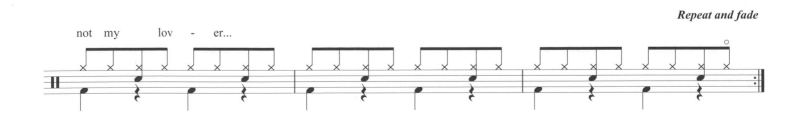

Blinding Lights

Words and Music by Abel Tesfaye, Max Martin,
Jason Quenneville, Oscar Holter and Ahmad Balshe

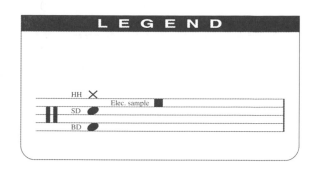

Intro
Fast ♩ = 171

Play 3 times

Verse

I've been try - na   call...

Pre-Chorus

Sin Cit-y's cold and emp - ty...

Play 3 times

Chorus

Ooh,   I'm   blind - ed by   the lights...

1., 2.   3.

I'm run-ning out of

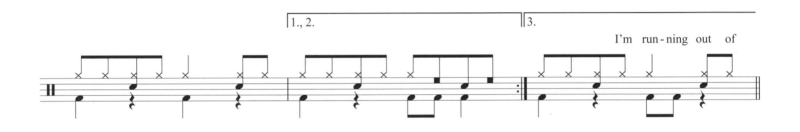

1.

Verse

time...

2.

Pre-Chorus

The   cit - y's   cold   and   emp - ty...

Play 3 times

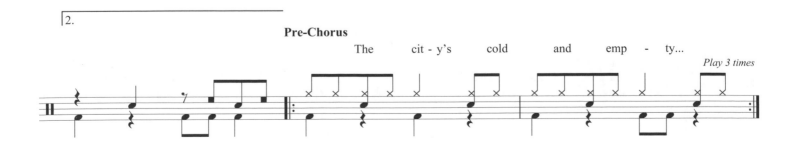

Chorus
Ooh,

I'm   blind - ed   by   the lights...

1., 2., 3.

4.

Outro

9

Can't Stop the Feeling!

Words and Music by Justin Timberlake, Max Martin and Shellback

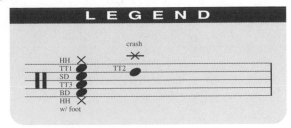

Verse

Oo,   it's some-thing mag - i - cal...

Play 3 times

Pre-Chorus

Play 4 times   *Play 4 times*

Chorus

|1., 3. |2.

Castle on the Hill

Words and Music by Ed Sheeran and Benjamin Levin

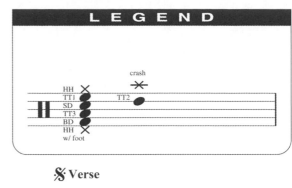

Intro
Moderately fast ♩ = 135

𝄋 **Verse**

When I was six years old...

...I

Pre-Chorus

found my heart...

Play 3 times

Chorus

I'm on my way...

Play 3 times

To Coda ⊕

D.S. al Coda
(take repeats)

⊕ **Coda**

Interlude

3

Verse

One   friend   left   to   sell   clothes...

$p < mf$

*Play crashes very lightly, next 7 meas.

Chorus

I'm on my way...

...when we did not know the an - swers...

Outro

Fade out

Circles

Words and Music by Austin Post, Kaan Gunesberk,
Louis Bell, William Walsh and Adam Feeney

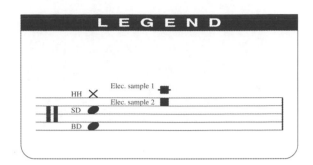

Intro
Moderately ♩ = 120

Play 4 times

Verse

We could-n't turn   a-round...

Play 4 times

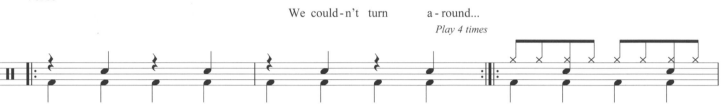

Play 3 times

𝄋 Chorus

Sea-sons changed   and our   love went   cold...

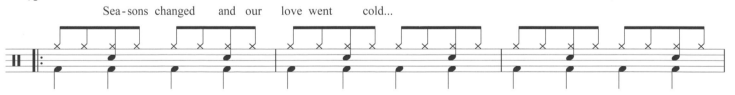

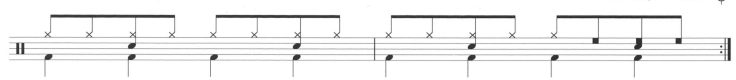

Verse

Let   go,   I got a feel - ing that it's time to let   go...

Play 5 times

D.S. al Coda 1
(take repeat)

⊕ **Coda 1**

Bridge

Make up your mind...

| **3** |

D.S. al Coda 2   ⊕ **Coda 2**

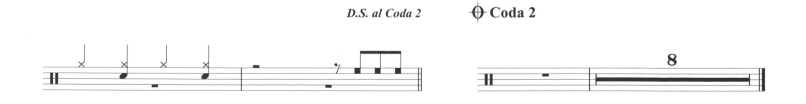

8

Crazy

Words and Music by Brian Burton, Thomas Callaway,
GianPiero Reverberi and GianFranco Reverberi

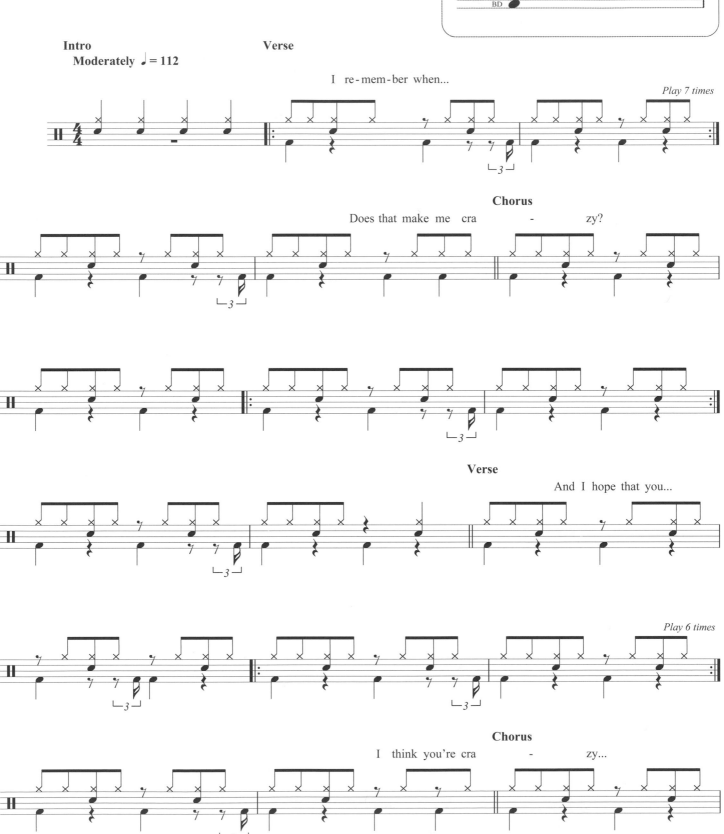

Verse

My he - roes had the heart...

Chorus

But may - be I'm cra - zy...

Outro

Crazy in Love

Words and Music by Beyonce Knowles,
Rich Harrison, Sean Carter and Eugene Record

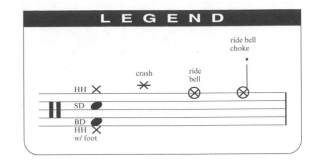

Intro
Moderate Hip-Hop ♩ = 100

Uh-oh, uh - oh, uh-oh, oh, no-no...

Play 3 times

Verse

I love to stare   so   deep in your eyes...

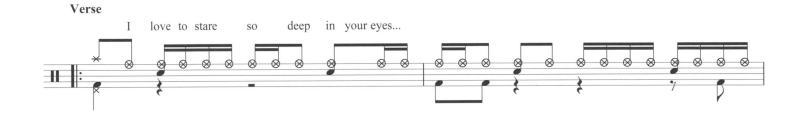

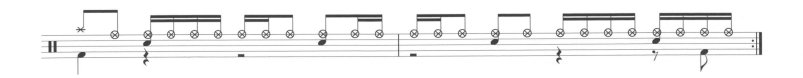

Chorus

Got me look - in' so cra - zy right now...

Play 4 times

Interlude/Verse

Uh - oh,   uh - oh,   uh - oh,   oh, no - no...

1., 2.   3.

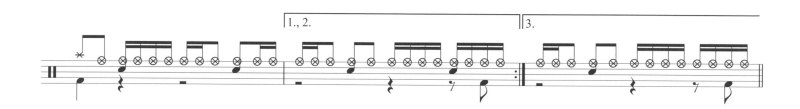

Chorus   **Verse**

Young Hov,   y'all   know...

Play 5 times

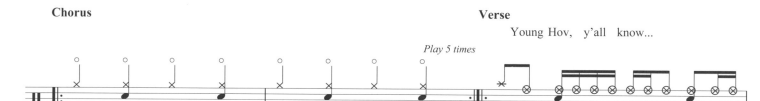

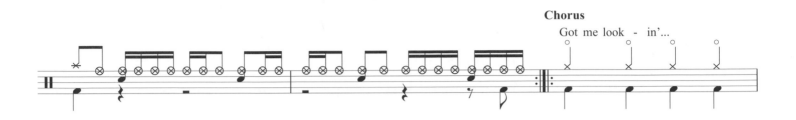

Chorus

Got me look - in'...

'Cause your love's

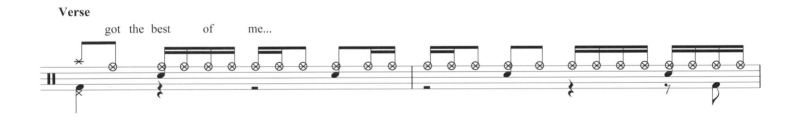

Verse

got the best of me...

Chorus

Got me look-in' so cra - zy right now...

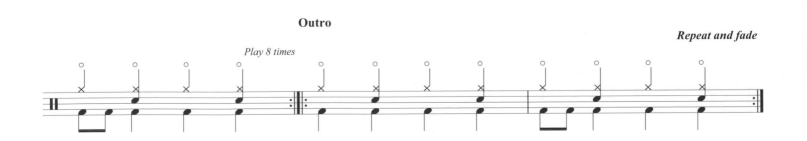

Outro

Repeat and fade

Play 8 times

Don't You (Forget About Me)

from the Universal Picture THE BREAKFAST CLUB
Words and Music by Keith Forsey and Steve Schiff

Intro
Moderately ♩ = 112

Verse

Won't   you   come   see   a - bout   me?

Chorus

Don't you ... for - get a - bout me...

Bridge

Will you stand a - bove me?

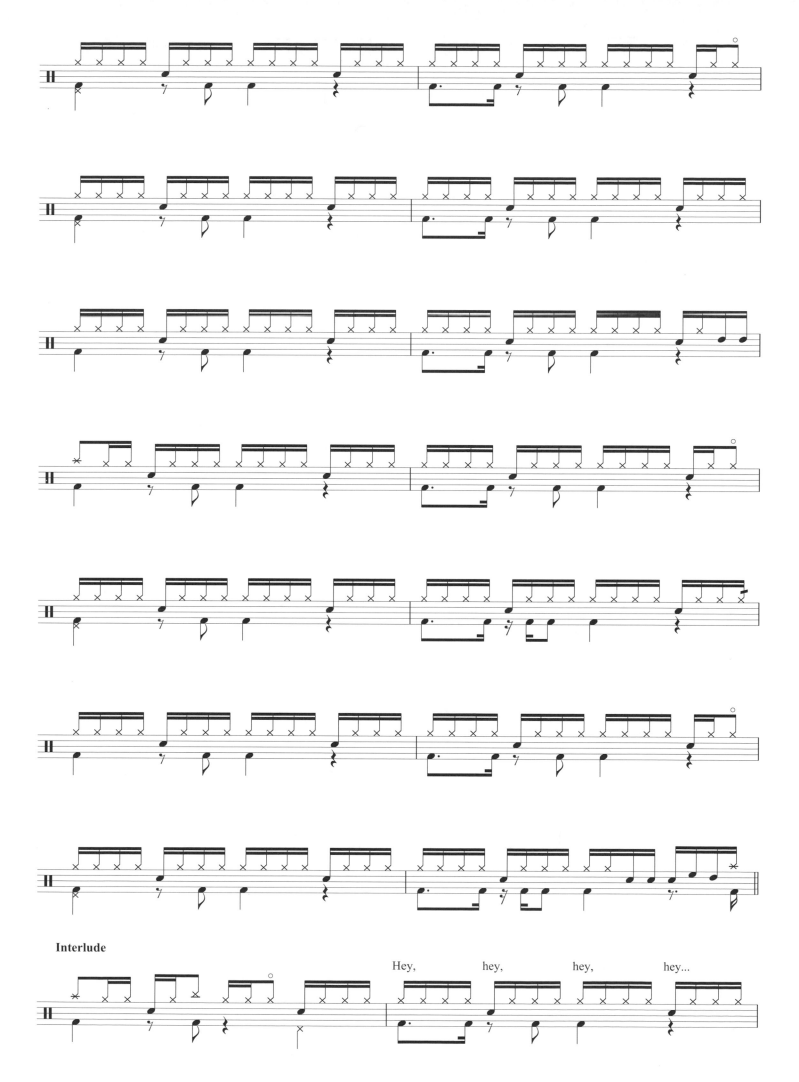

Interlude

Hey,   hey,   hey,   hey...

Verse

Don't   you   try   and   pre - tend...

Play 3 times

Chorus

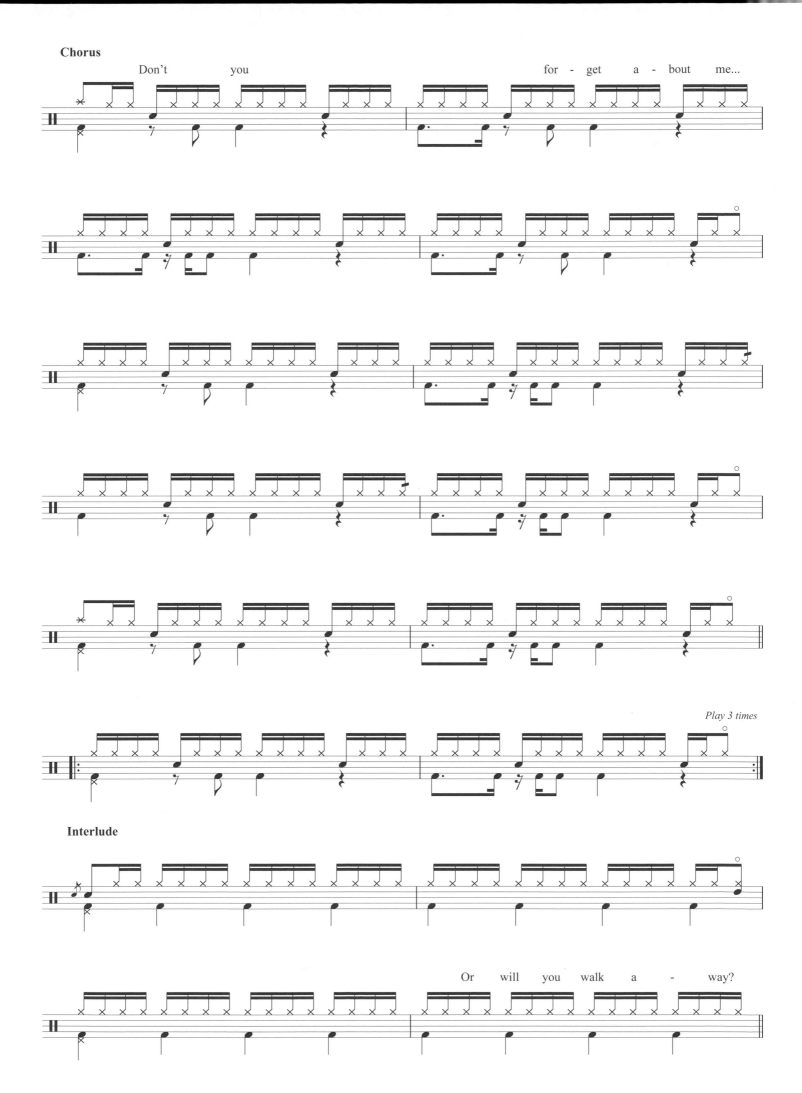

*Play D tom 2nd time.

I sing,

Outro

"La, la, la, la, la..."

Repeat and fade

Drops of Jupiter (Tell Me)

Words and Music by Pat Monahan, James Stafford,
Robert Hotchkiss, Charles Colin and Scott Underwood

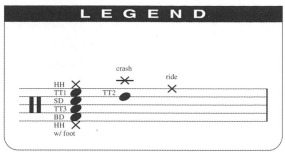

Chorus
tell   me...

Interlude

Can you im - ag - ine no

Bridge
love...

...and head back t'ward the Milk - y Way...

Outro

Na, na, na, na, na, na...

Play 3 times

poco rit.

Dynamite

Words and Music by Taio Cruz, Lukasz Gottwald,
Max Martin, Benjamin Levin and Bonnie McKee

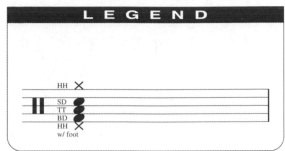

⊕ Coda

Bridge

I'm gon-na take it all...

Play 8 times

Pre-Chorus

I throw my hands up in the air some - times...

Chorus

...rock this club...

Play 4 times

Every Breath You Take

Music and Lyrics by Sting

Intro
Moderate Rock ♩ = 114

Play 3 times

Verse

Ev - 'ry breath   you   take...

Play 4 times

Verse

Play 3 times

𝄋 **Chorus**

Oh,   can't   you   see?

Play 3 times

Verse

Ev - 'ry move   you   make...

To Coda ⊕

Play 3 times

Bridge

Since you've gone...

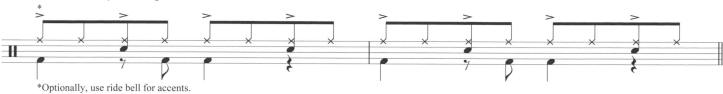

*Optionally, use ride bell for accents.

Play 3 times

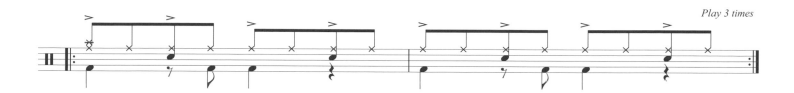

Interlude

Play 3 times   *Play 3 times*

D.S. al Coda
(take repeats)

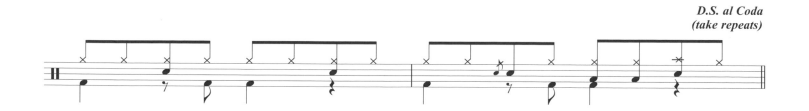

41

Coda

Ev-'ry move you make...

I'll be watch - ing

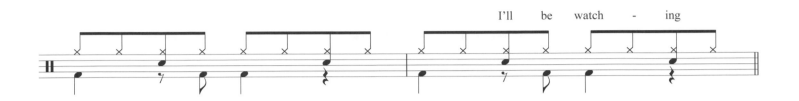

Outro

you...

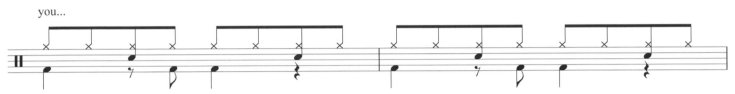

I'll be watch - ing

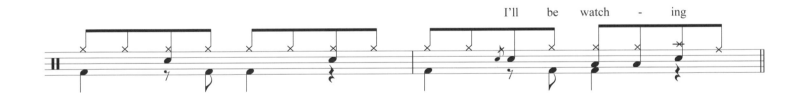

you.

Repeat and fade

I'll be watch - ing

Girls Just Want to Have Fun

Words and Music by Robert Hazard

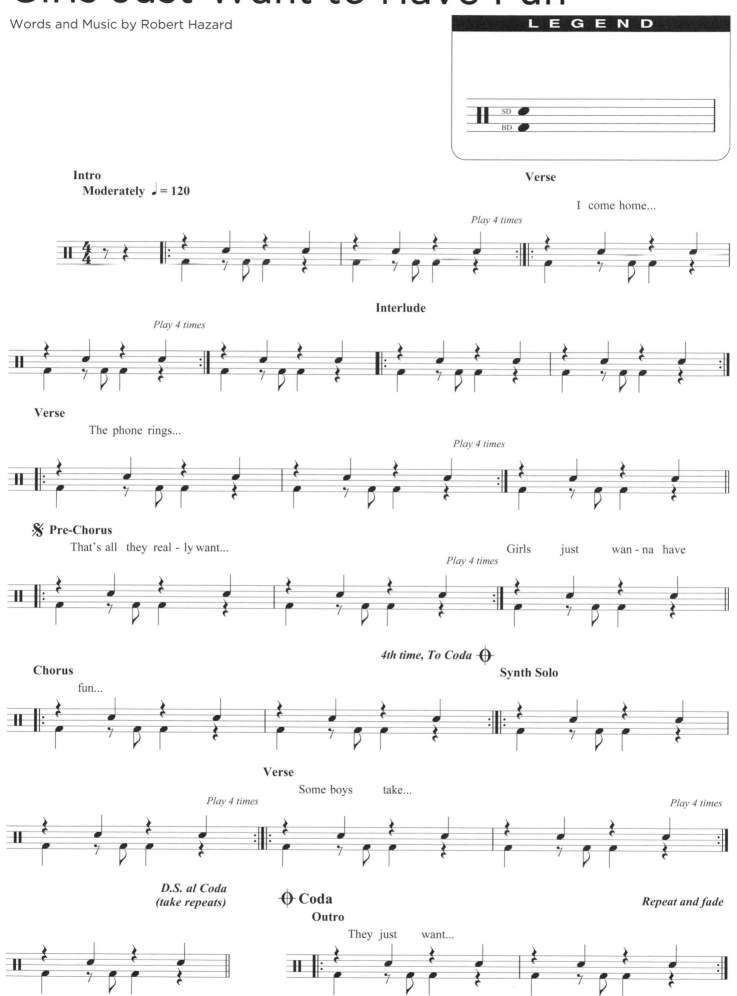

Everybody Wants to Rule the World

Words and Music by Ian Stanley,
Roland Orzabal and Christopher Hughes

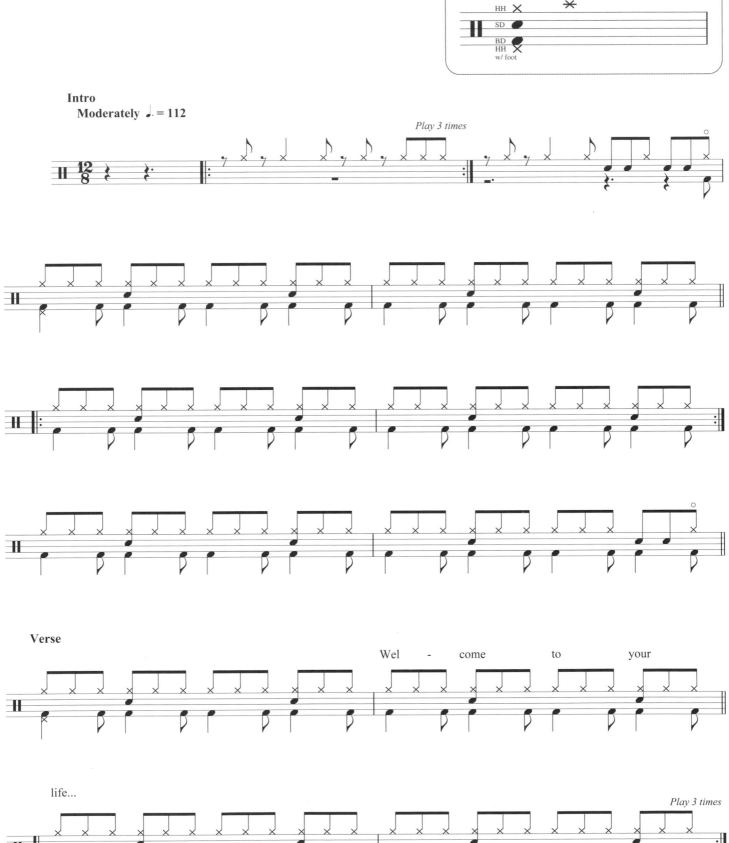

Chorus

Ev - 'ry - bod - y wants to rule the

Interlude

world...

Play 3 times

Verse

It's my own de -

sign...

Chorus

Ev - 'ry - bod - y wants to rule the

Bridge

world.   There's   a   room...

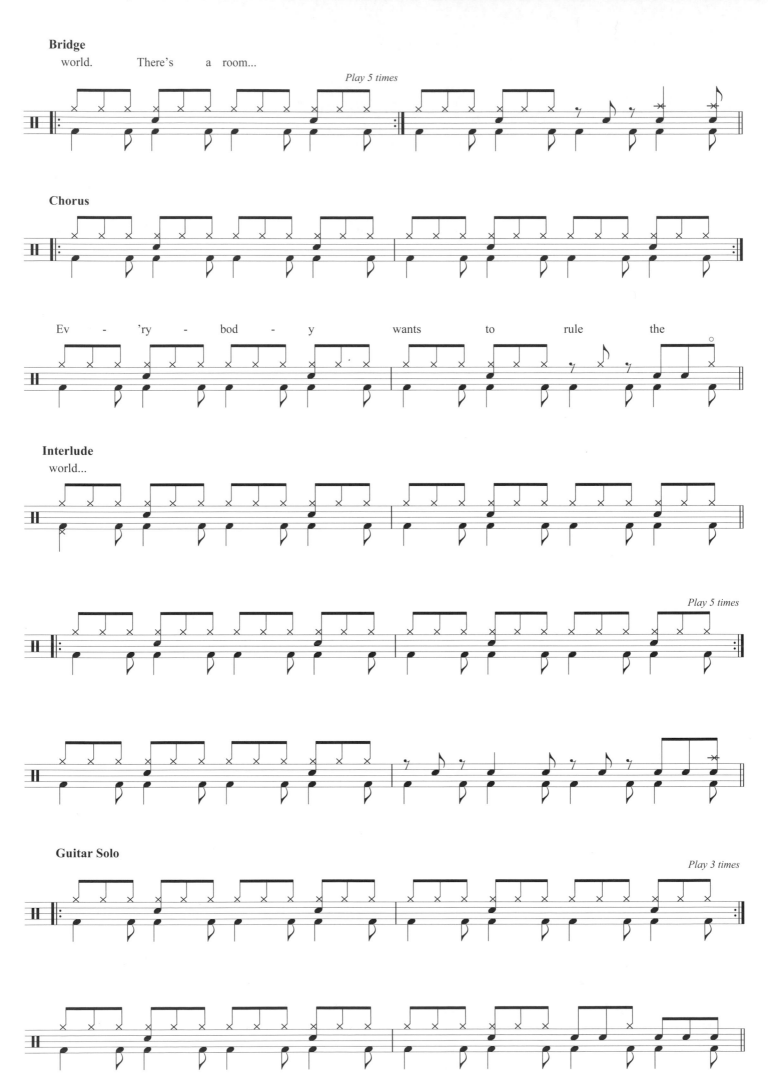

Fallin'

Words and Music by Alicia Keys

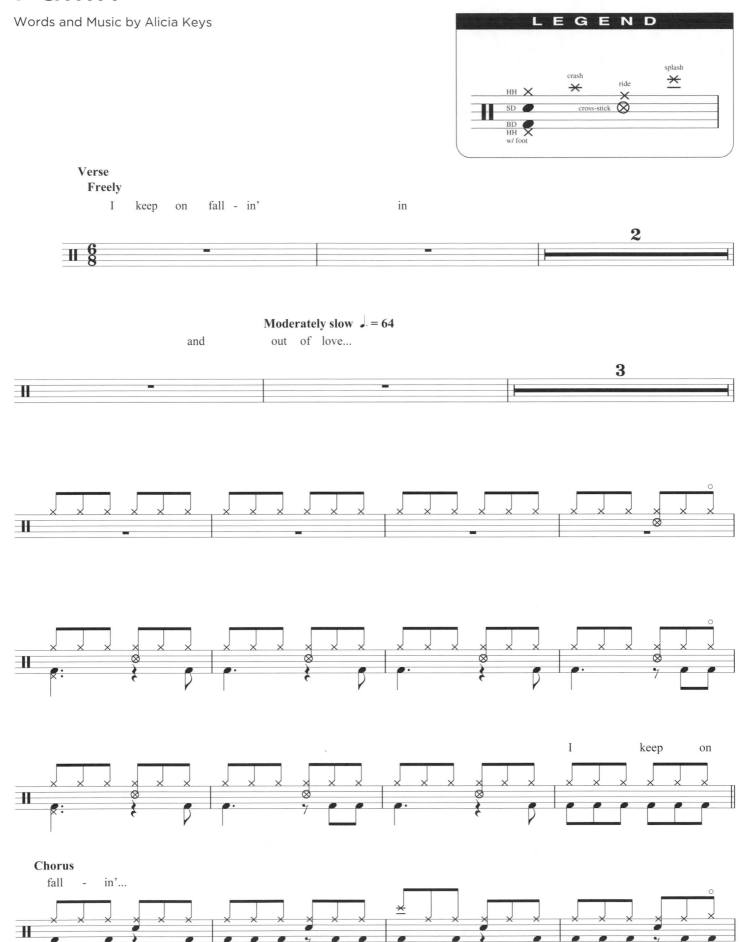

Oh,   oh,

Verse
I   nev - er felt this   way...

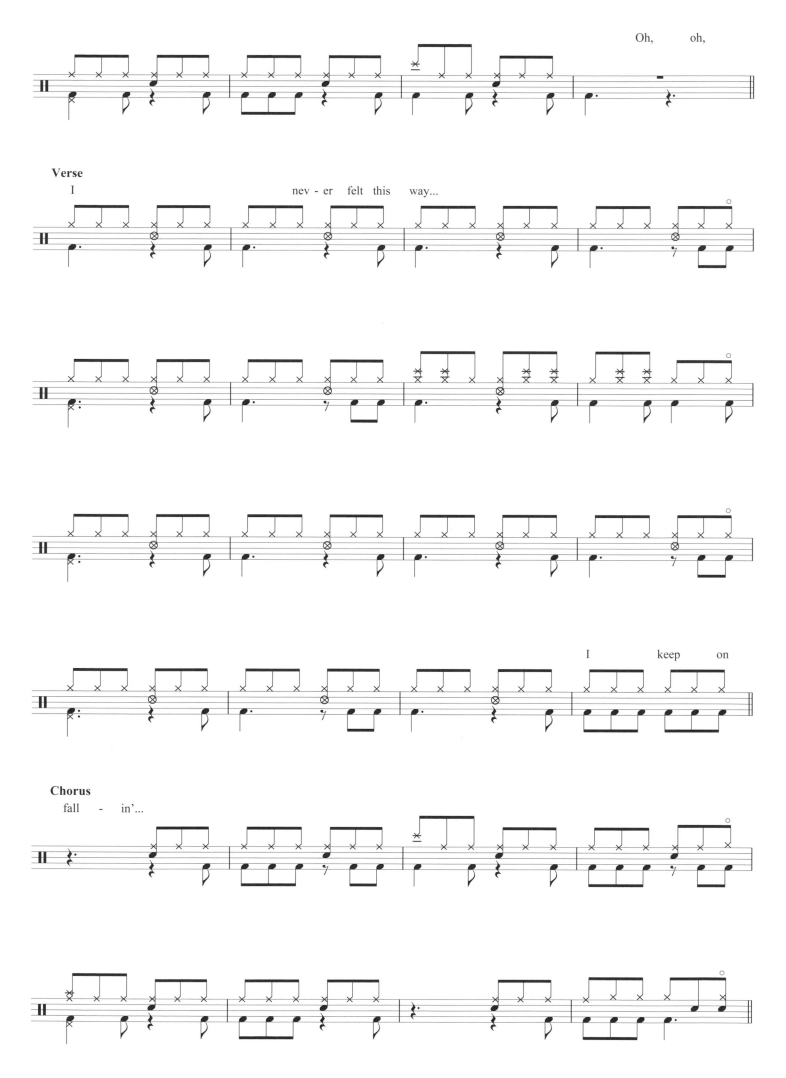

I   keep   on

Chorus
fall   -   in'...

Interlude

I keep on

Chorus

fall - in'...

50

Outro

Fifty Ways to Leave Your Lover

Words and Music by Paul Simon

Intro
Moderately ♩ = 102

Play 3 times

Verse

The prob-lem is all in-side your head...

Play 7 times

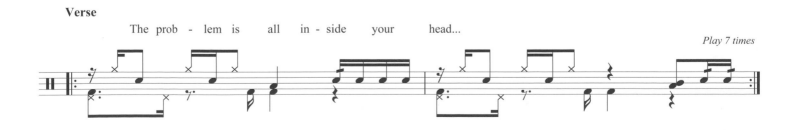

You just slip out the

Chorus
back, Jack...

Verse

She said, "It   grieves me   so...

Play 3 times

Play 3 times

You just slip out the

Chorus

back,   Jack...

Outro   *Repeat and fade*

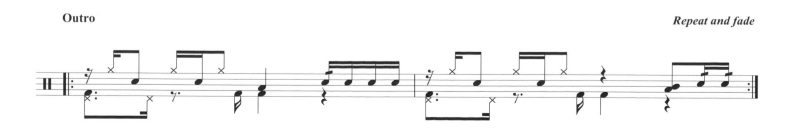

Get Lucky

Words and Music by Thomas Bangalter,
Guy Manuel Homem Christo, Nile Rodgers and Pharrell Williams

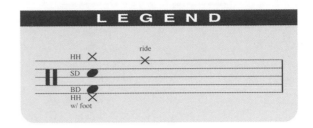

Chorus

She's up   all   night till the sun...

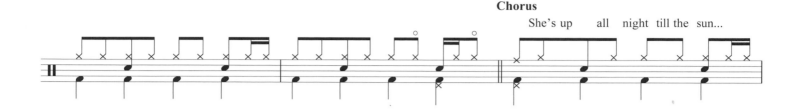

To Coda ⊕

Interlude

D.S. al Coda

The pre-sent has   no   rib -

Coda

We're up all night till the sun...

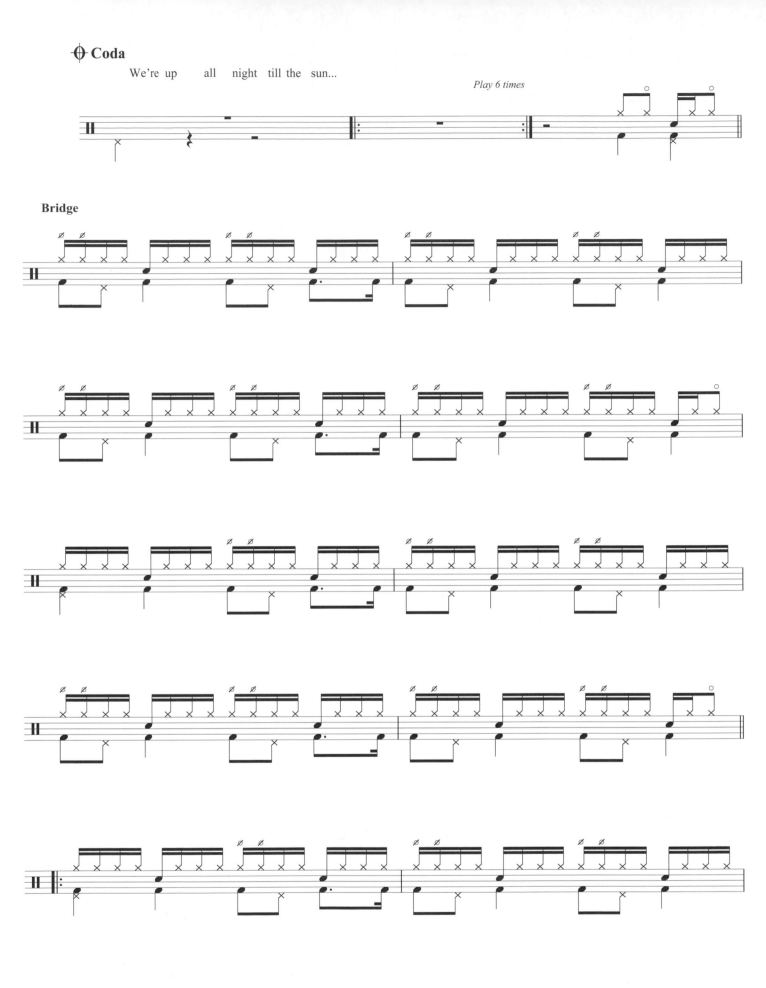

Bridge

Pre-Chorus

We've   come   too   far...

Chorus

She's up   all   night   till the   sun...

1., 2., 3.

4.

Outro

Begin fade   *Fade out*

Gimme All Your Lovin'

Words and Music by Billy F Gibbons,
Dusty Hill and Frank Lee Beard

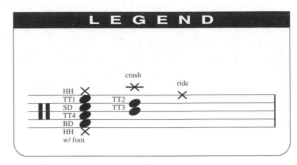

Intro
Moderate Rock ♩ = 120

Play 4 times

Verse

...have a shot...

Chorus

Gim - me all your lov - in'...

You got - ta

Play 3 times

Verse

whip it up...

Play 3 times

Chorus

Gim - me all your lov - in'...

Guitar Solo

*Optionally, use HH throughout Guitar Solos.

Verse

You got - ta   move it up...

Play 3 times

Chorus

Gim - me all your lov - in'...

Interlude

Outro-Guitar Solo

Repeat and fade

Play 3 times

Happy

from DESPICABLE ME 2
Words and Music by Pharrell Williams

Intro
Moderately fast ♩ = 160

%Verse

It might seem cra - zy what I'm 'bout to say...

Play 7 times

Chorus

Be - cause I'm hap - py...

To Coda ⊕

Play 7 times

D.S. al Coda
(take repeats)

⊕ Coda

Bridge

Bring me down, can't noth - in'...

Play 8 times

Chorus

Bridge

Bring me down, can't noth - in'...

Play 16 times

Play 8 times

Chorus

Play 15 times

Levitating

Words and Music by Dua Lipa, Stephen Kozmeniuk,
Clarence Coffee Jr. and Sarah Hudson

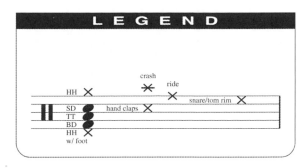

Intro
Moderately ♩ = 103

Verse

If you wan-na run...

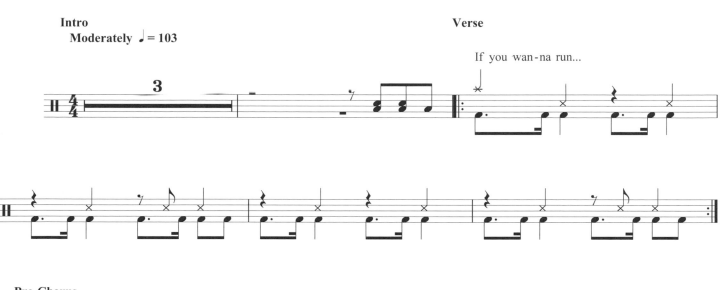

Pre-Chorus

You want me...

Chorus

I got you...

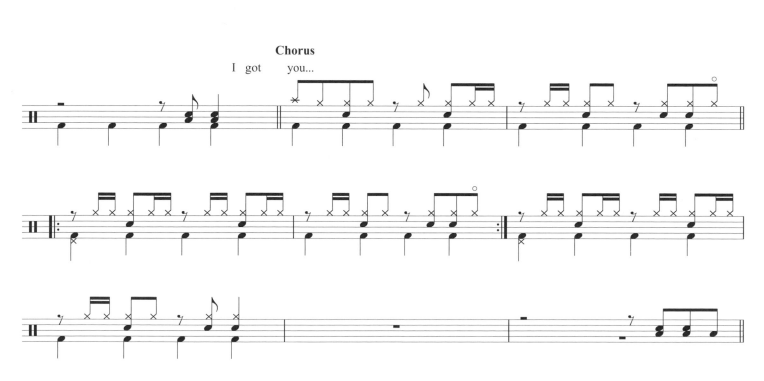

Verse

I be-lieve that you're for me...

Pre-Chorus

You want me...

Chorus

I got you...

You can fly a-way...

Play 3 times

Bridge

...love is like a rock-et...

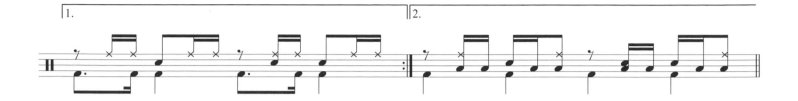

Pre-Chorus

You want me...

Chorus

You can fly a-way...

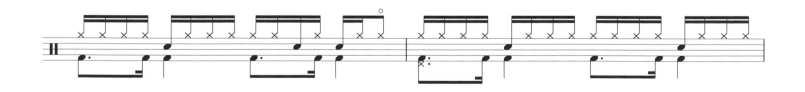

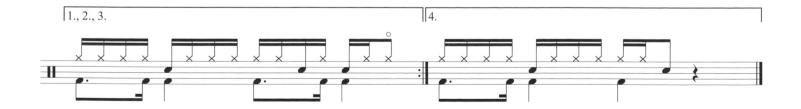

Heathens

from SUICIDE SQUAD
Words and Music by Tyler Joseph

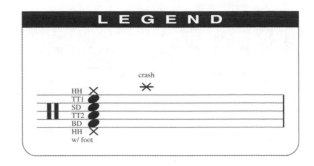

Intro-Chorus
Moderately slow ♩ = 90

All my friends are heath-ens; take it slow...

Chorus
All my friends are heath-ens; take it slow...

Play 3 times

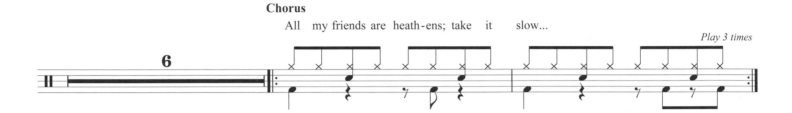

Verse
Wel-come to the room...

Chorus
All my friends are heath-ens; take it slow...

Play 3 times

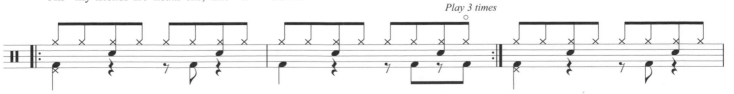

Verse

We don't deal with...

Interlude

Chorus

Please   don't make   an - y   sud - den

moves...

Play 4 times

Outro-Chorus

Why'd you come? You knew you should have   stayed...

I Need to Know

Words and Music by Cory Rooney and Marc Anthony

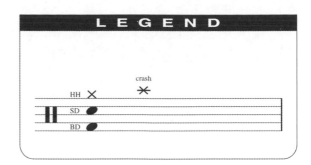

Intro
Moderately ♩ = 115

Verse
They say   a-round...

𝄋 **Pre-Chorus**
If   it's   true...

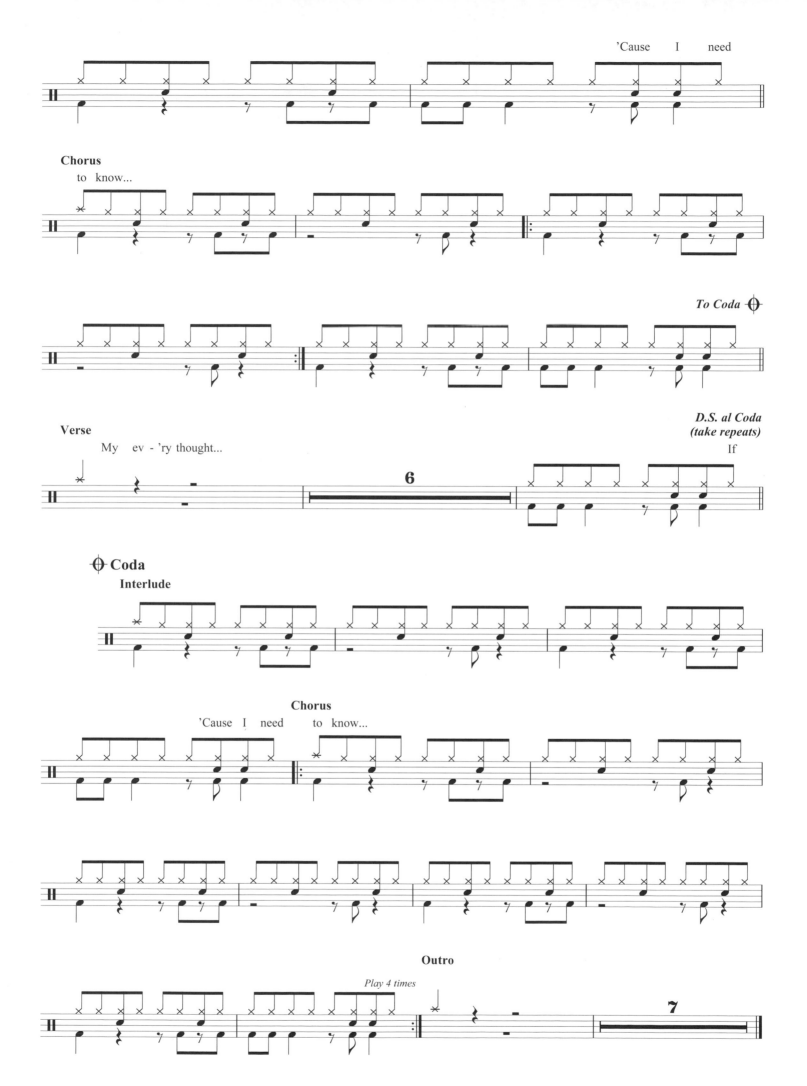

Juice

Words and Music by Lizzo, Theron Makiel Thomas,
Eric Frederic, Sam Sumser and Sean Small

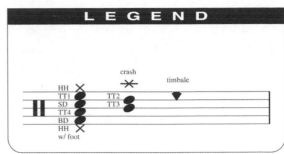

Chorus

It ain't my fault...

1.

2.

Verse

No, I'm not a snack at all...

How I

Chorus

It ain't my fault...

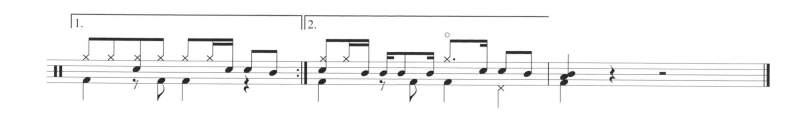

Jump

Words and Music by Edward Van Halen,
Alex Van Halen and David Lee Roth

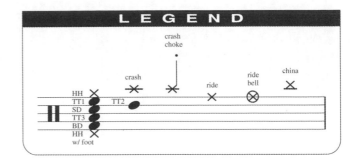

Intro
Moderately fast ♩ = 130

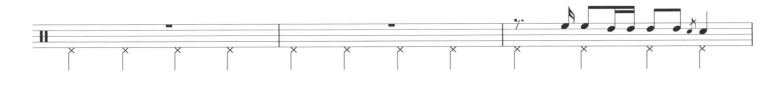

Play 4 times

Pre-Chorus

Ah, can't you   see me stand-ing here...

Chorus

Ah,   might as   well   jump...

Verse

Pre-Chorus

Chorus

Guitar Solo

Synth Solo

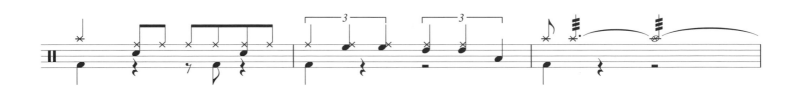

Interlude

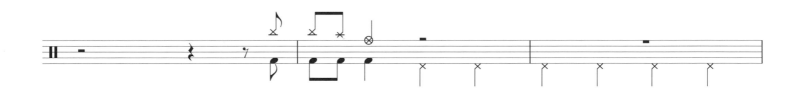

Might as   well   jump...

Outro-Chorus

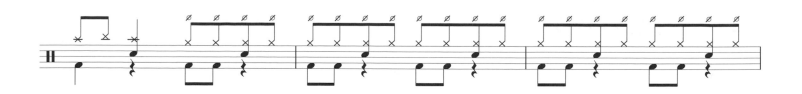

Begin fade

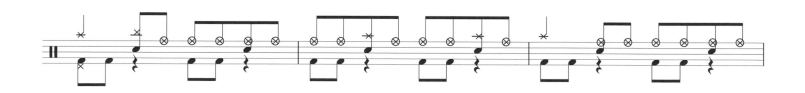

Fade out

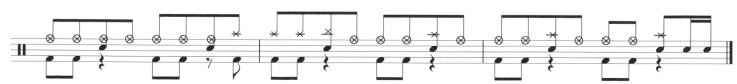

Just Dance

**Words and Music by Stefani Germanotta,
RedOne and Aliaune Thiam**

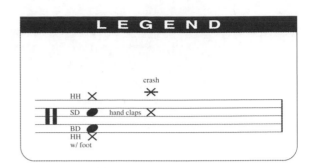

**Intro
Moderately** ♩ = 119

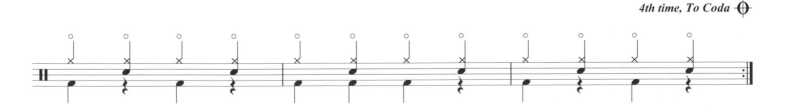

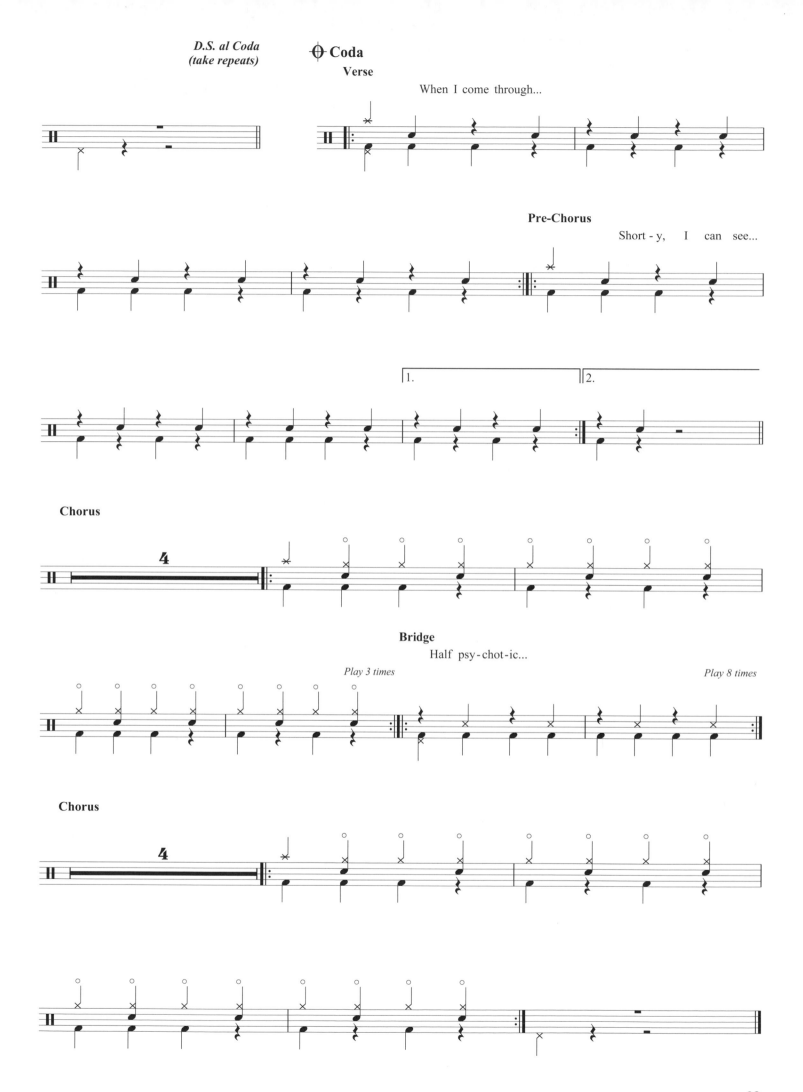

Livin' La Vida Loca

Words and Music by Desmond Child and Robi Rosa

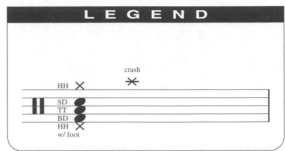

Intro
Fast ♩ = 178

Verse

She's in - to su - per - sti - tions...

Interlude

Verse

She's in - to new sen - sa - tions...

𝄋 Pre-Chorus

She'll make you take your clothes off...

Chorus

Up - side,   in -

- side   out...

Play 3 times

8th time, To Coda ⊕

Play 4 times

Interlude

Verse

Woke   up   in

85

New York   Cit - y...

D.S. al Coda
(take repeats)

Coda

Interlude

Play 4 times

Pre-Chorus

...make   you   take   your   clothes   off...

Play 4 times

Chorus

Up   -   side,   in   -   side   out...

Livin' on a Prayer

Words and Music by Jon Bon Jovi,
Desmond Child and Richie Sambora

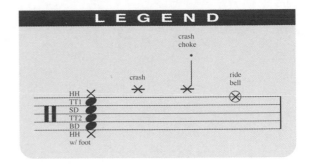

Intro
Moderate Rock ♩ = 122

(Keyboard)   14 sec.   (Bass)   **3**

Play 3 times

Verse
Tom - my used to work on the docks...

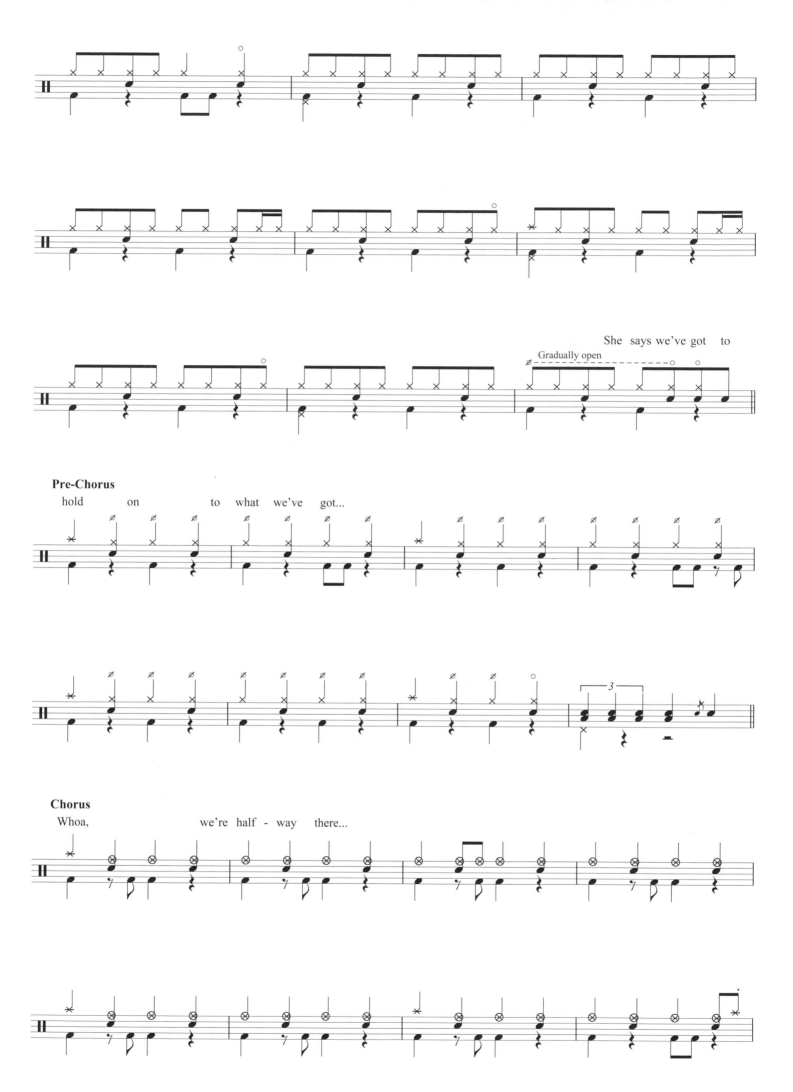

Pre-Chorus

Chorus

Verse
Tom-my's got his six-string in hock...

We've got to

Pre-Chorus
hold on to what we've got...

Chorus

Whoa,   we're half - way   there...

Guitar Solo

Outro-Chorus

Whoa,   we're half - way   there...

Begin fade

Fade out

Pride (In the Name of Love)

Words and Music by U2

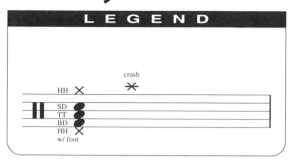

*Floor tom placed to left of hi-hat and played with left-hand stick.

Intro
Moderately ♩ = 105

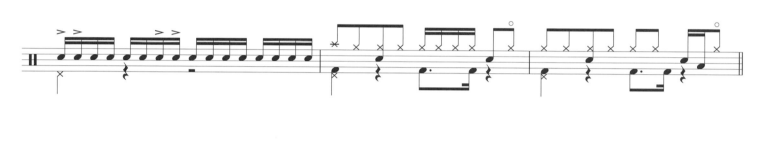

Verse

One man   come   in   the   name   of   love...

Play 3 times

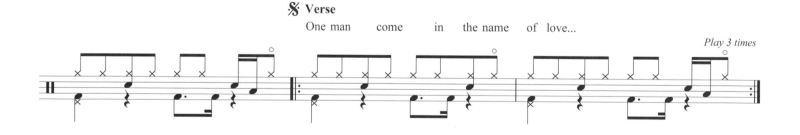

In   the   name

Chorus

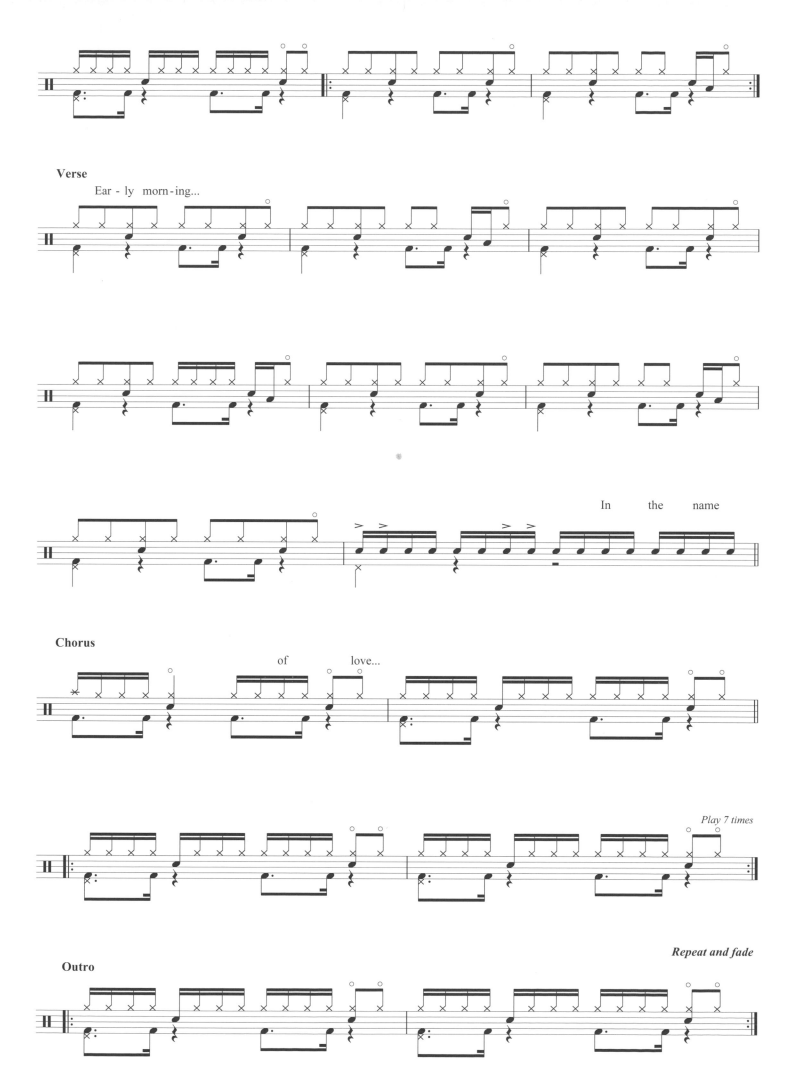

Verse

Ear - ly morn-ing...

In   the   name

Chorus

of   love...

Play 7 times

Repeat and fade

Outro

Mercy

Words and Music by Aimee Duffy and Stephen Booker

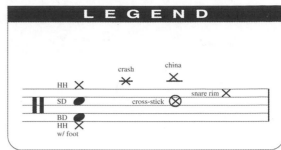

Intro
Moderately fast ♩ = 130

Yeah,   yeah,   yeah...

Play 6 times

Verse

...you,   but I   got - ta stay...   ...mer - cy.

Chorus

Play 8 times

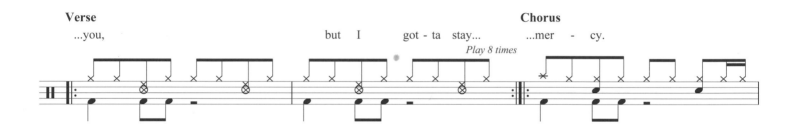

Why won't   you re - lease   me?

Play 3 times

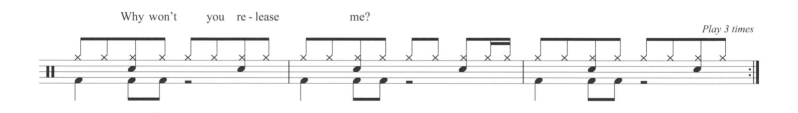

Verse   **Chorus**

...will be some - thin'...   ...mer - cy.

Play 8 times

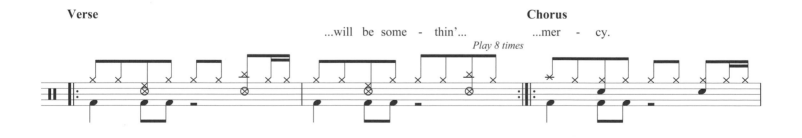

Why won't   you re - lease   me?

Play 3 times

Bridge

I'm beg-gin' you for mer - cy...

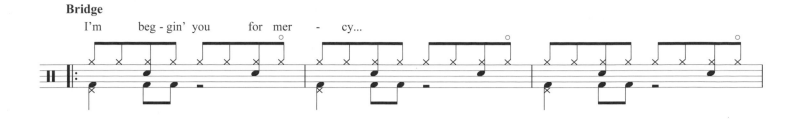

Chorus

Mer - cy.   Why won't   you re - lease   me?

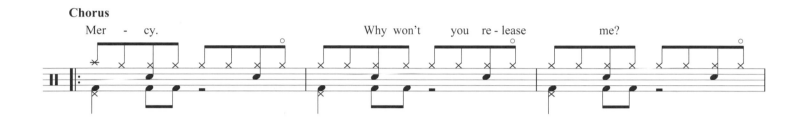

Outro

Play 6 times

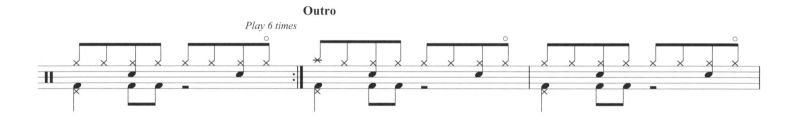

Repeat and fade

I'm beg-gin' you for mer - cy...

Moves Like Jagger

Words and Music by Adam Levine,
Benjamin Levin, Ammar Malik and Shellback

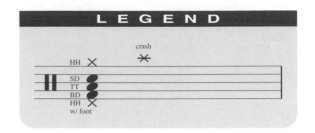

Chorus

Take me by the tongue,

and I'll know you.

Verse

You wan - na know...

Chorus

Take me by the tongue, and I'll know you.

Outro

Only Wanna Be With You

Words and Music by Darius Rucker,
Dean Felber, Mark Bryan and Jim Sonefeld

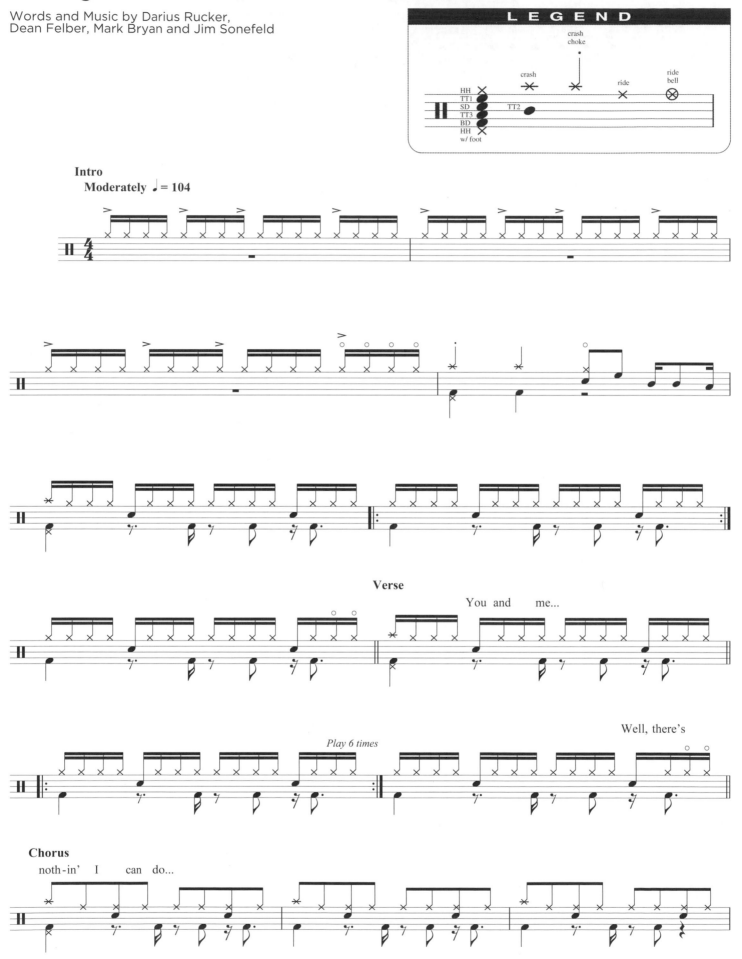

Verse

You look at me...

Well, there's

Chorus

noth-in' I can do...

Put on a lit-tle Dyl - an...

Verse

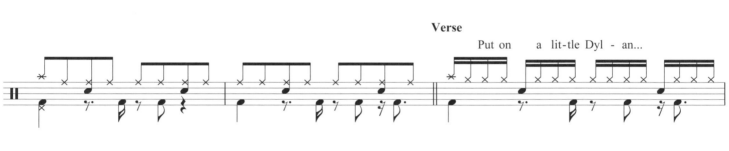

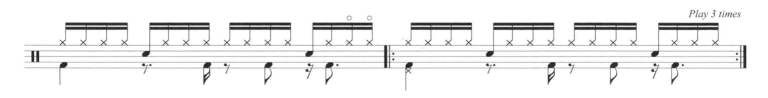

Chorus

I can't help it if I'm luck - y...

Guitar Solo

Yeah, I'm

Chorus

tang-led up in blue...

Interlude

Verse

Some - times I won - der...

Play 3 times

Chorus

noth-in' I   can   do...

Well, there's

Outro

poco rit.

Pour Some Sugar on Me

Words and Music by Joe Elliott, Phil Collen,
Richard Savage, Richard Allen, Steve Clark and R.J. Lange

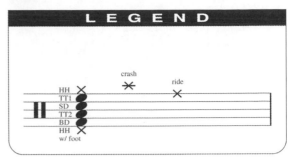

Intro
Moderate Rock ♩ = 85

Play 3 times

Verse

Love is like a bomb...

1.

2.

℅ Pre-Chorus

Take a bot - tle...

Chorus

Pour some sug - ar on me...

To Coda

Interlude

Play 3 times

Verse

Lis - ten, red light, yel - low light, green light, go...

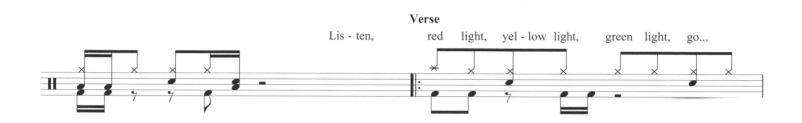

1. 2.

D.S. al Coda
(take repeat)

Coda

Interlude

Bridge

You got   the peach - es...

Pre-Chorus

Take a bot - tle...

Chorus

Pour some sug - ar on me...

Roar

Words and Music by Katy Perry, Max Martin,
Dr. Luke, Bonnie McKee and Henry Walter

Intro
Moderately slow ♩ = 90

Verse

I used to bite my tongue and hold my breath...

Play 4 times

Pre-Chorus

Play 4 times

Chorus

Play 7 times

Verse

Now I'm float - in' like   a but - ter - fly...

Pre-Chorus

Play 4 times

Chorus

Play 7 times

Play 7 times

Interlude

pp

f

Chorus

Play 7 times

Play 7 times

Rude

Words and Music by Nasri Atweh, Mark Pellizzer,
Alex Tanas, Ben Spivak and Adam Messinger

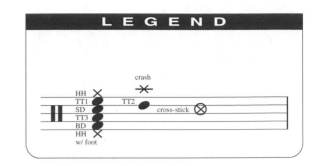

Verse
Moderately fast ♩ = 144

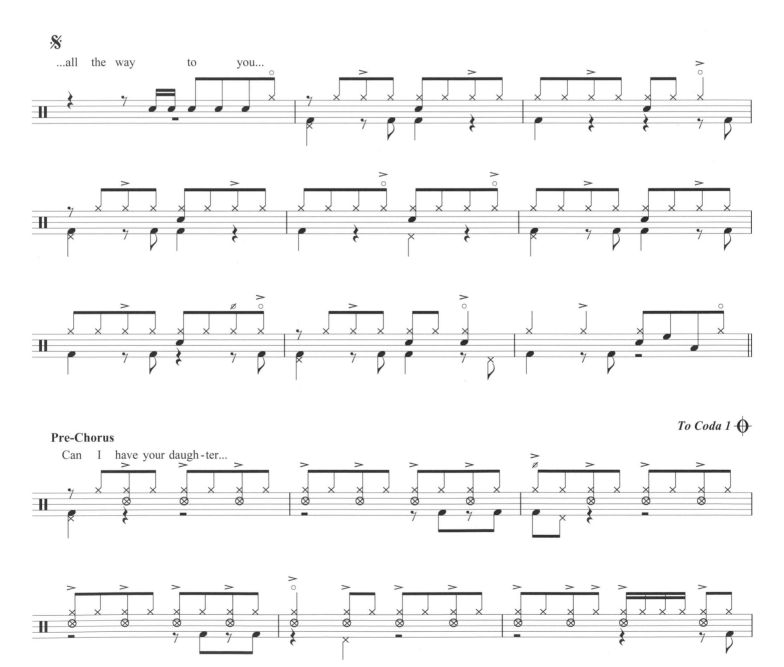

Interlude

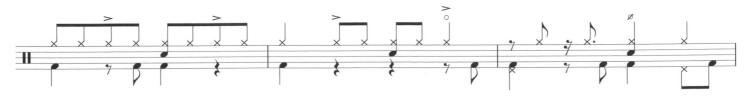

D.S. al Coda 1

Verse

I   hate   to...

$\oplus$ **Coda 1**

D.S.S. al Coda 2

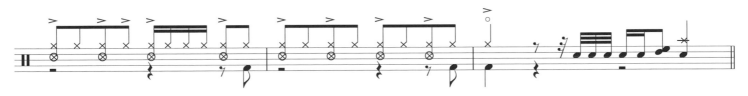

$\oplus$ **Coda 2**

Interlude-Guitar Solo

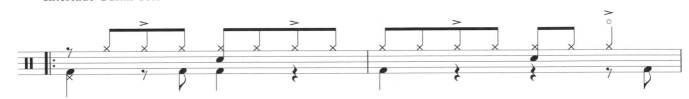

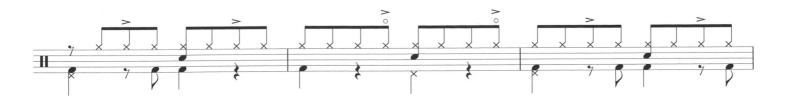

D.S.S. al Coda 3

Pre-Chorus

Can   I   have your daugh-ter...

Coda 3

...be   so   rude...

Send My Love (To Your New Lover)

Words and Music by Adele Adkins, Max Martin and Shellback

Intro
Moderately ♩ = 82

Verse

This was all   you...

Play 4 times

Pre-Chorus

I'm   giv - ing you   up...

Chorus

Send my love   to your new   lov - er...

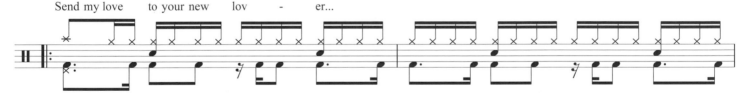

Verse

I was too strong...

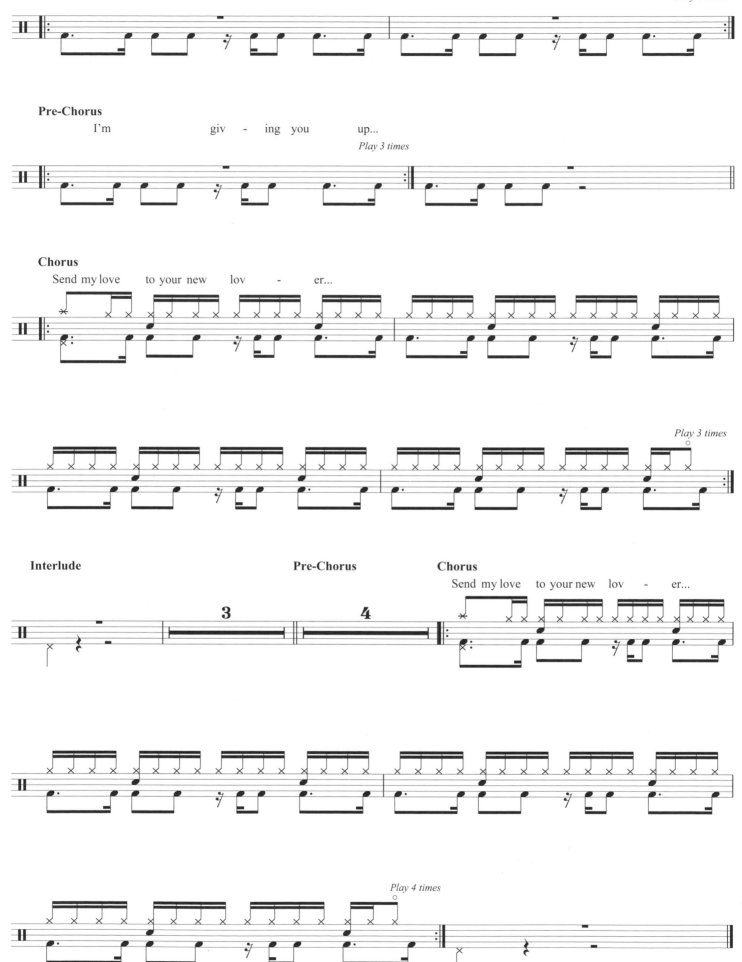

Play 4 times

Pre-Chorus

I'm giv - ing you up...

Play 3 times

Chorus

Send my love to your new lov - er...

Play 3 times

Interlude   **Pre-Chorus**   **Chorus**

Send my love to your new lov - er...

Play 4 times

Separate Ways
(Worlds Apart)

Words and Music by Steve Perry and Jonathan Cain

Chorus

Some - day,   love   will   find   you...

Play 3 times

Play 3 times

Interlude

Verse

Trou-bled   times...

1., 2., 3.

4.

Pre-Chorus

If you must   go...

Chorus

Some - day,   love   will   find   you...

Play 3 times

Play 3 times

Guitar Solo

sim. throughout

Interlude

Play 3 times

Chorus

Some - day,   love   will   find   you...

Play 3 times

Play 3 times

Outro

I still

love you, girl...

No...

Smooth

Words by Rob Thomas
Music by Rob Thomas and Itaal Shur

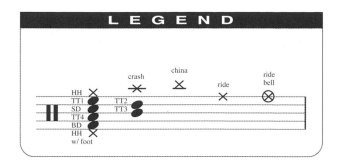

Intro
Moderately ♩ = 116

Verse
hot   one...

Pre-Chorus
And if you said this life...

And it's

Chorus
just like the o - cean...

Interlude

But I'll tell you

Verse

one   thing...

Pre-Chorus

And if you said   this   life...

And it's

Chorus

just like the o - cean...

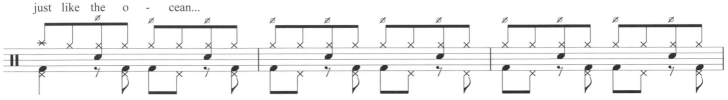

Guitar Solo

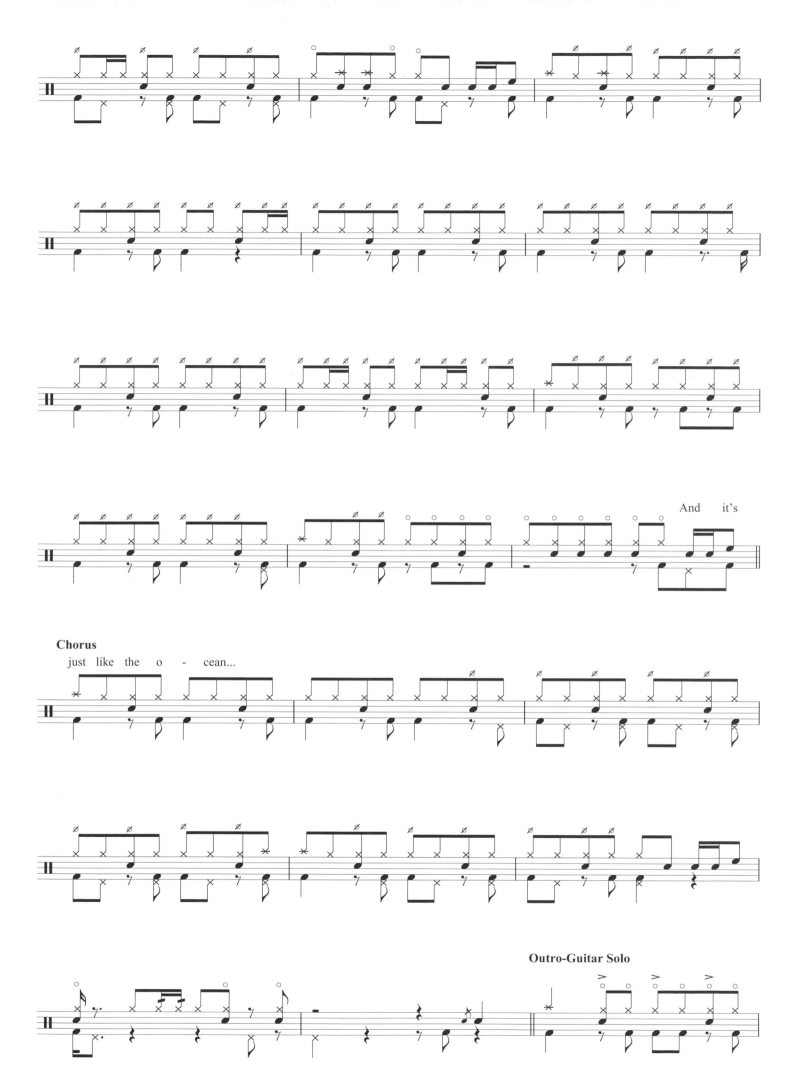

And it's

Chorus
just like the o - cean...

Outro-Guitar Solo

Or else for-get a-bout it...

Begin fade

Fade out

Shut Up and Dance

Words and Music by Ryan McMahon, Ben Berger,
Sean Waugaman, Eli Maiman, Nicholas Petricca and Kevin Ray

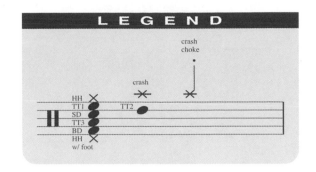

Pre-Chorus

She took my arm...

To Coda ⊕

Chorus

"Oh, don't you dare look back, just keep your eyes on me."

Interlude

Verse

A back - less dress and some beat - up sneaks...

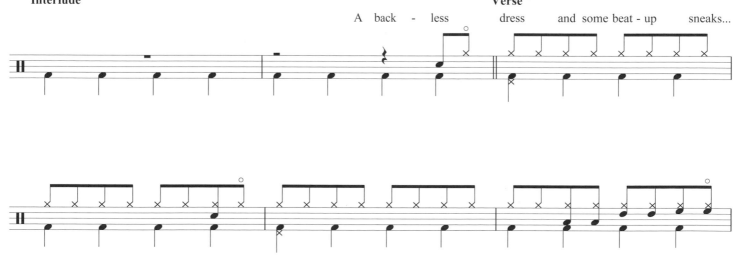

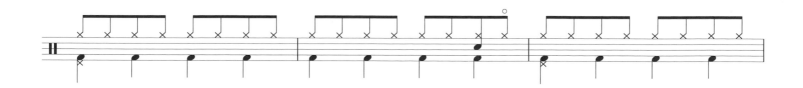

Pre-Chorus

She took my arm...

D.S. al Coda

 Coda

Synth Solo

Pre-Chorus

Deep in her eyes...

130

Interlude

Play 3 times

"Oh, don't you

Chorus

dare look back,   just keep your eyes on   me."

Play 3 times

Chorus

1.

2.

3.

Stayin' Alive

from the Motion Picture SATURDAY NIGHT FEVER
Words and Music by Barry Gibb, Robin Gibb and Maurice Gibb

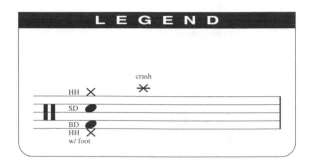

Intro
Moderate Disco ♩ = 104

Verse
Well, you can tell...

Pre-Chorus
...al - right, it's o - kay...

Chorus
Wheth-er you're a broth-er...

Stay-in' a-live...

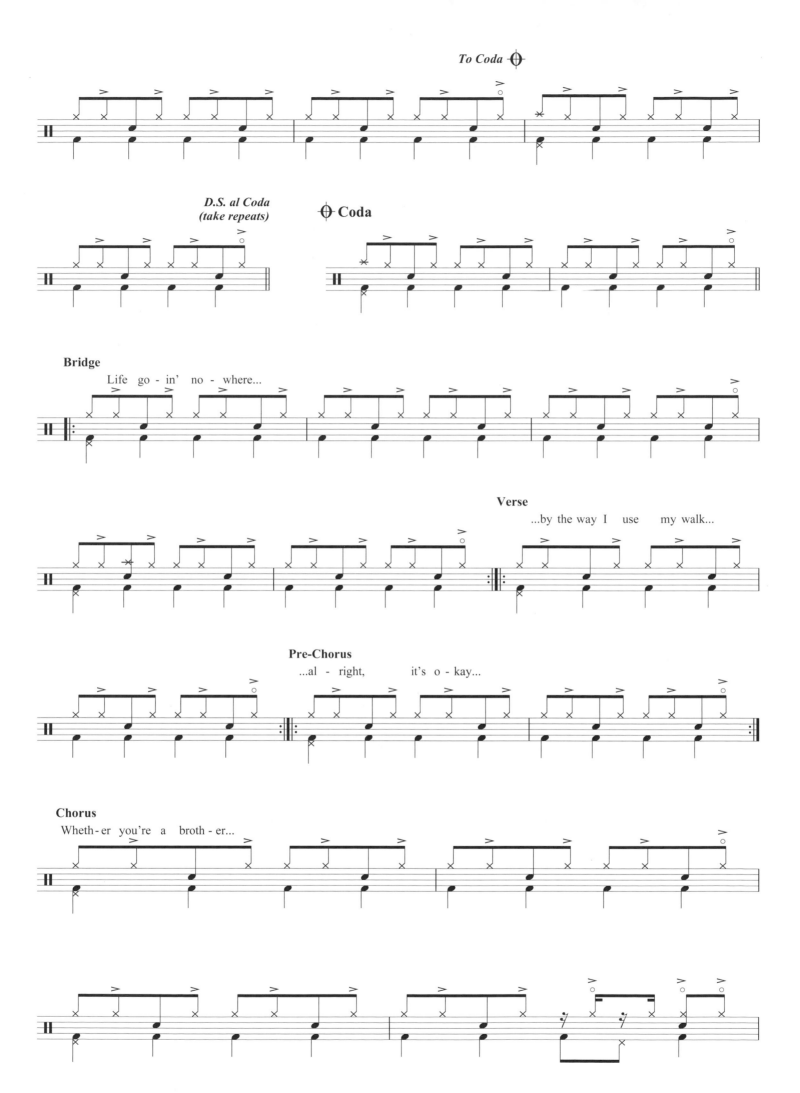

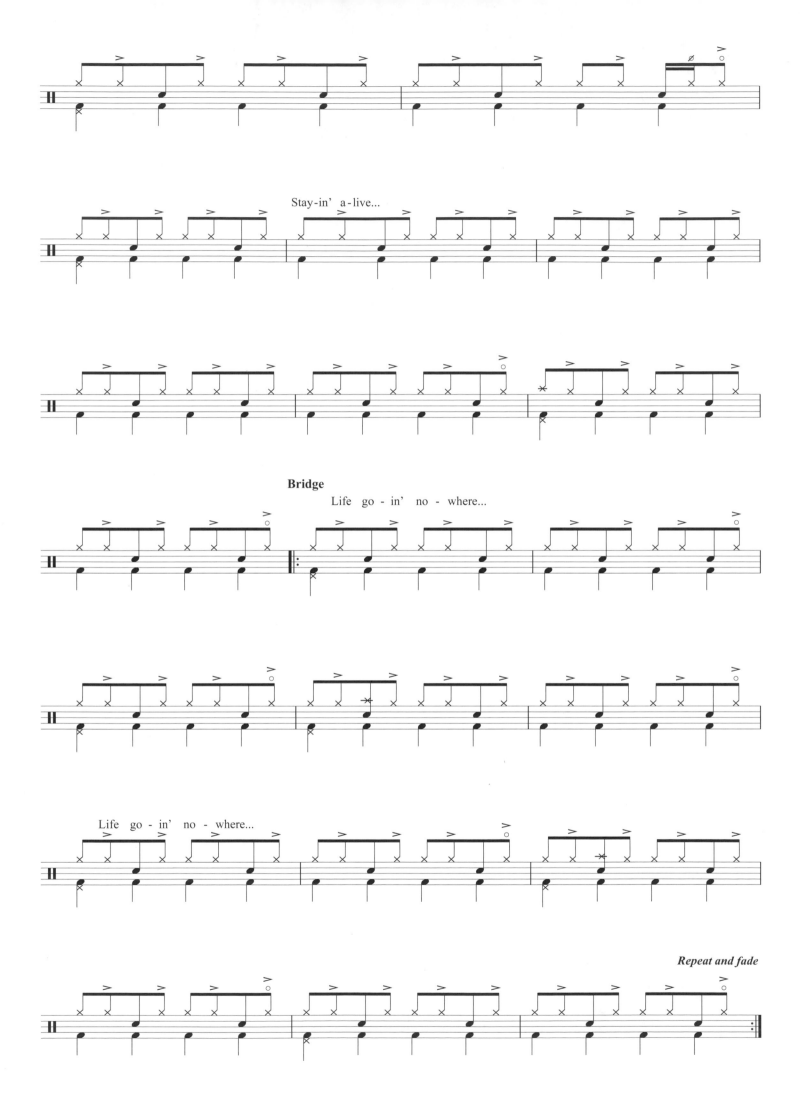

Stay-in' a-live...

Bridge

Life go - in' no - where...

Life go - in' no - where...

Repeat and fade

Valerie

Words and Music by Sean Payne, David McCabe,
Abigail Harding, Boyan Chowdhury and Russell Pritchard

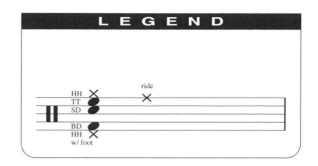

Intro
Fast ♩ = 212

Verse
Well, some - times...

Play 7 times

Pre-Chorus
'Cause since I've come...

Play 6 times

Why don't you come on o - ver, Val -

7th time, To Coda

Chorus
- e - rie...

Play 4 times

Verse

...have to go to jail...

Play 3 times

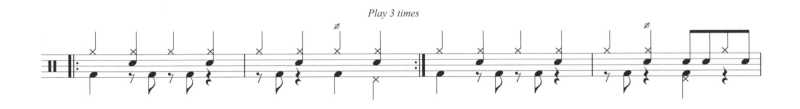

D.S. al Coda
(take repeats)

Coda

Verse

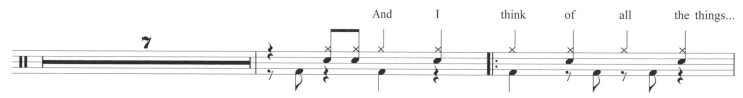

Pre-Chorus

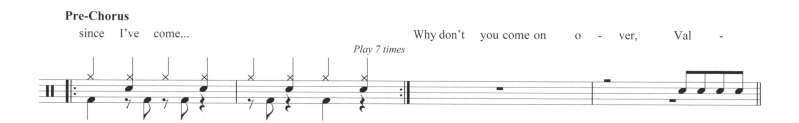

Chorus

Stronger (What Doesn't Kill You)

Words and Music by Greg Kurstin,
Alexandra Tamposi, David Gamson and Jorgen Elofsson

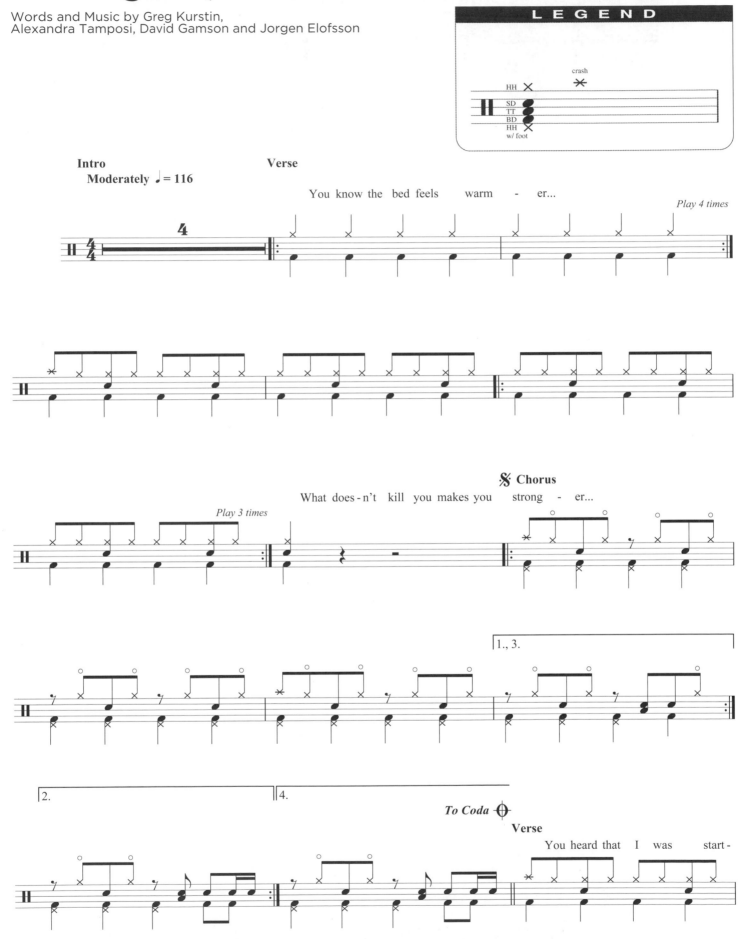

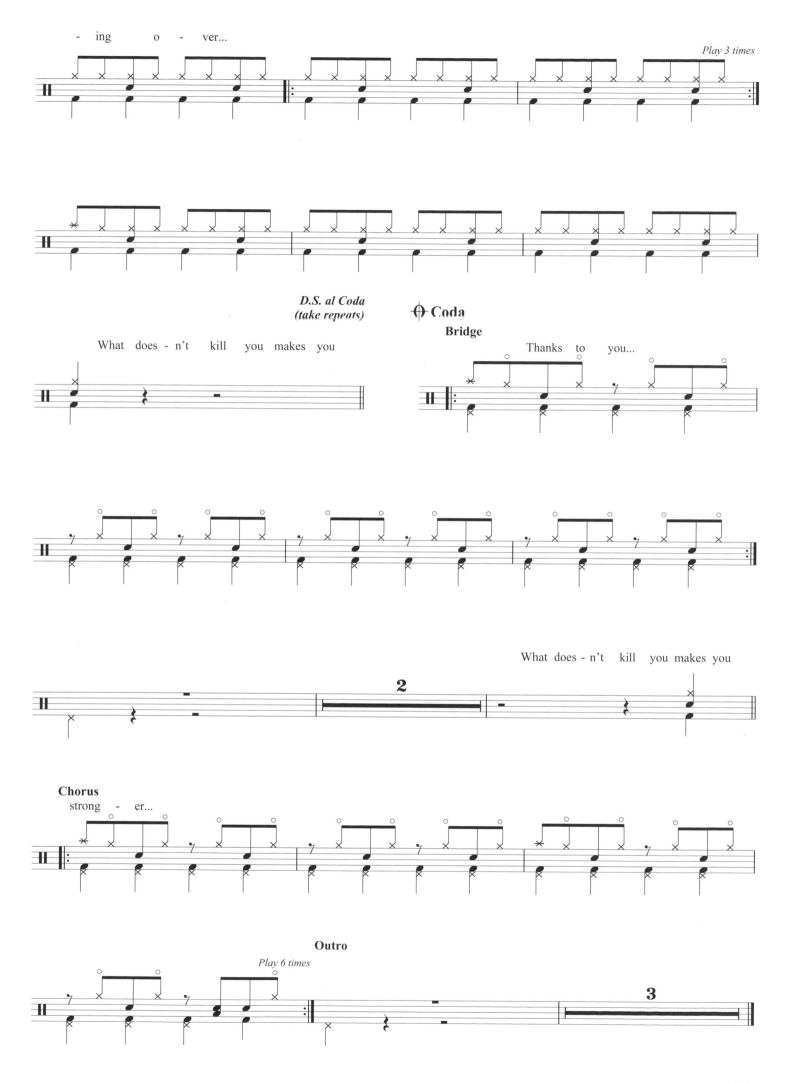

Umbrella

Words and Music by Shawn Carter,
Thaddis L. Harrell, Christopher Stewart and Terius Nash

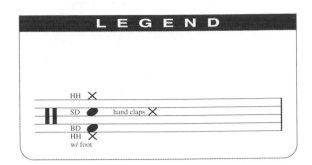

Intro
Moderately ♩ = 87

Uh-huh,   uh-huh...

Play 4 times

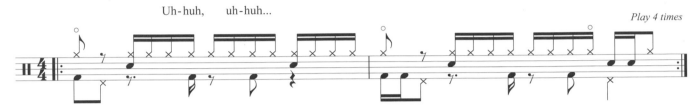

You know me...

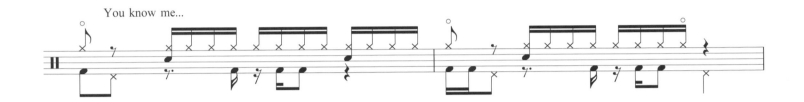

You

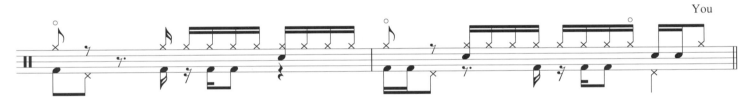

Verse

had   my heart...

Play 4 times

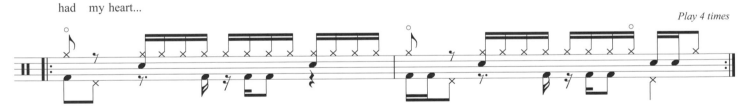

Pre-Chorus

When the sun   shine...

Play 4 times

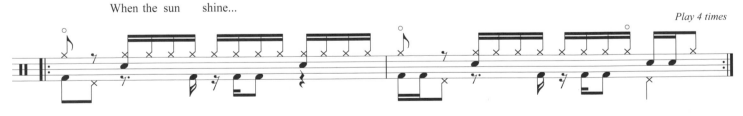

Chorus

...el - la,   el - la,   eh,   eh,   eh...

Play 4 times

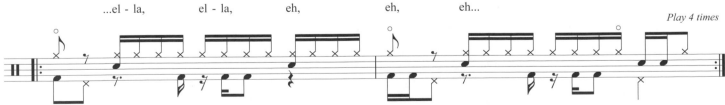

Verse

...fan - cy things...

Play 4 times

Pre-Chorus

When the sun   shine...

Play 4 times

Chorus

...el - la,   el - la,   eh,   eh,   eh...

Play 4 times

Bridge

You   can   run   in - to   my   arms...

Play 3 times

Be - cause

Pre-Chorus

when the sun   shine...

Play 4 times

Chorus

...el - la,   el - la,   eh,   eh,   eh...

Play 4 times

Repeat and fade

Outro

...rain - in',   rain - in'...

Uptown Funk

Words and Music by Mark Ronson, Bruno Mars, Philip Lawrence,
Jeff Bhasker, Devon Gallaspy, Nicholaus Williams, Lonnie Simmons,
Ronnie Wilson, Charles Wilson, Rudolph Taylor and Robert Wilson

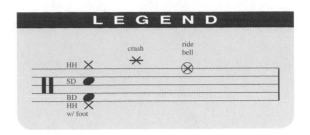

Intro
Moderately ♩ = 115

Verse
This hit, that ice cold...

Pre-Chorus

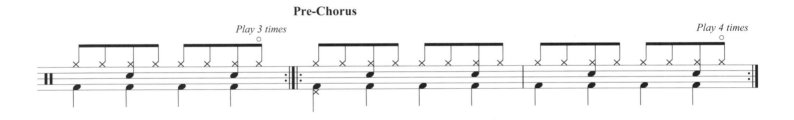

Chorus
Girls hit you, hal-le-lu-jah...

Interlude

Verse

Stop!   Wait a min - ute.

Pre-Chorus

Chorus

Girls   hit   you, hal - le - lu - jah...

Interlude

Bridge

Play 3 times

Interlude

Play 3 times

Outro

Walking on Sunshine

Words and Music by Kimberley Rew

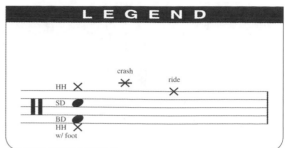

Intro
Fast ♩ = 220

Verse
...used to think...

Play 3 times

I just can't wait...

Play 3 times

Now I'm walk - in' on sun -

Chorus

- shine...

And don't it feel good...

I

Verse

used to think...

Play 3 times

I'm walk - in' on sun -

Chorus

- shine... And don't it feel good...

Play 5 times

Interlude

...I feel the love...

I'm walk - in' on sun -

Chorus

- shine... And don't it feel good...

Play 5 times

Outro

Repeat and fade

What Makes You Beautiful

Words and Music by Savan Kotecha, Rami Yacoub and Carl Falk

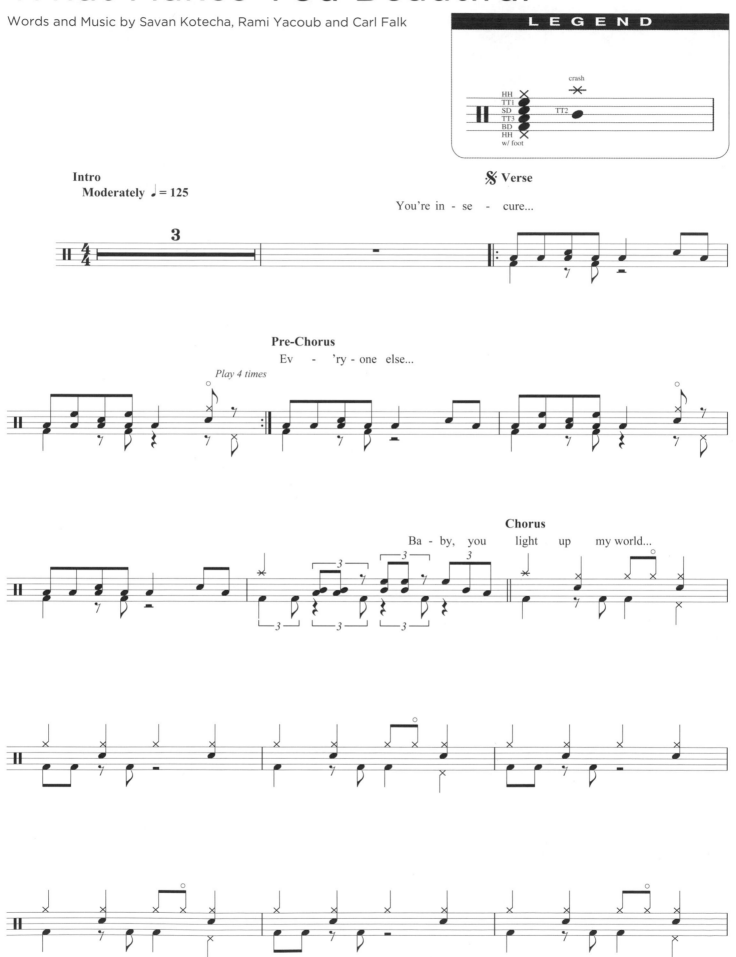

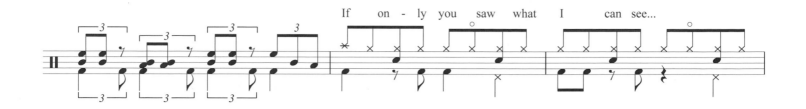

If on - ly you saw what I can see...

To Coda ⊕

That's what makes you beau - ti - ful...

D.S. al Coda
(take repeats)

So girl, come...

⊕ **Coda**

Interlude

Na, na, na, na...

Bridge

Ba - by, you...   Ba - by, you

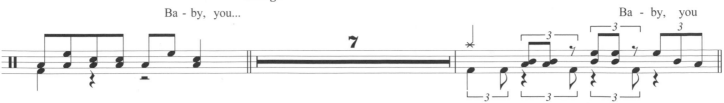

Chorus

light   up   my world...

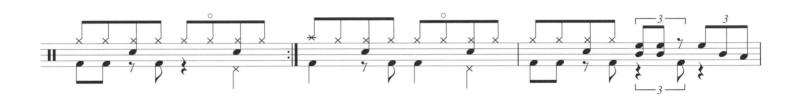

If   on - ly   you   saw   what   I   can   see...

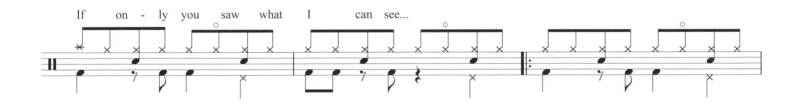

That's   what   makes   you   beau - ti - ful...

Who Knew

Words and Music by Alecia Moore,
Max Martin and Lukasz Gottwald

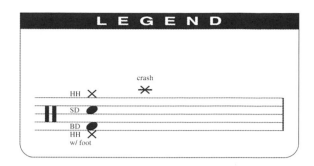

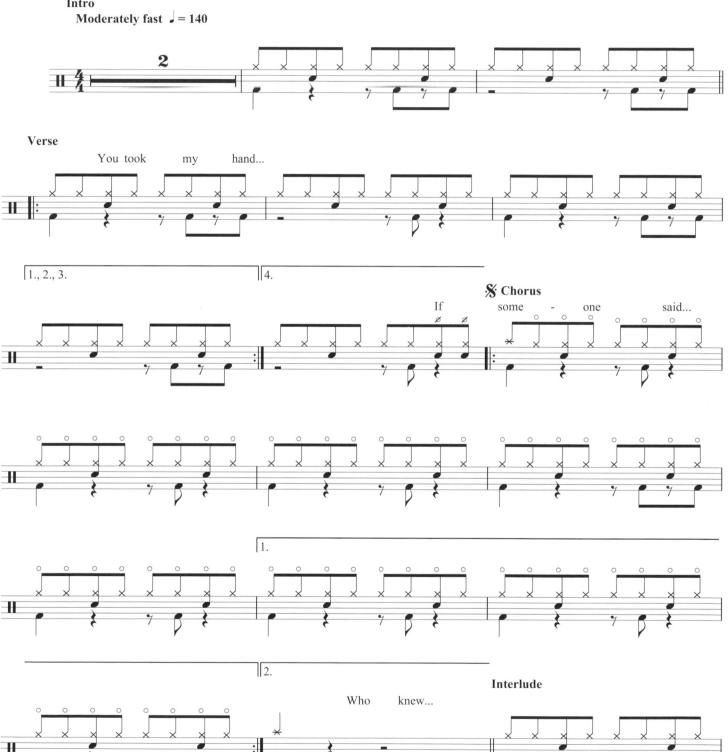

Who   knew...

Outro

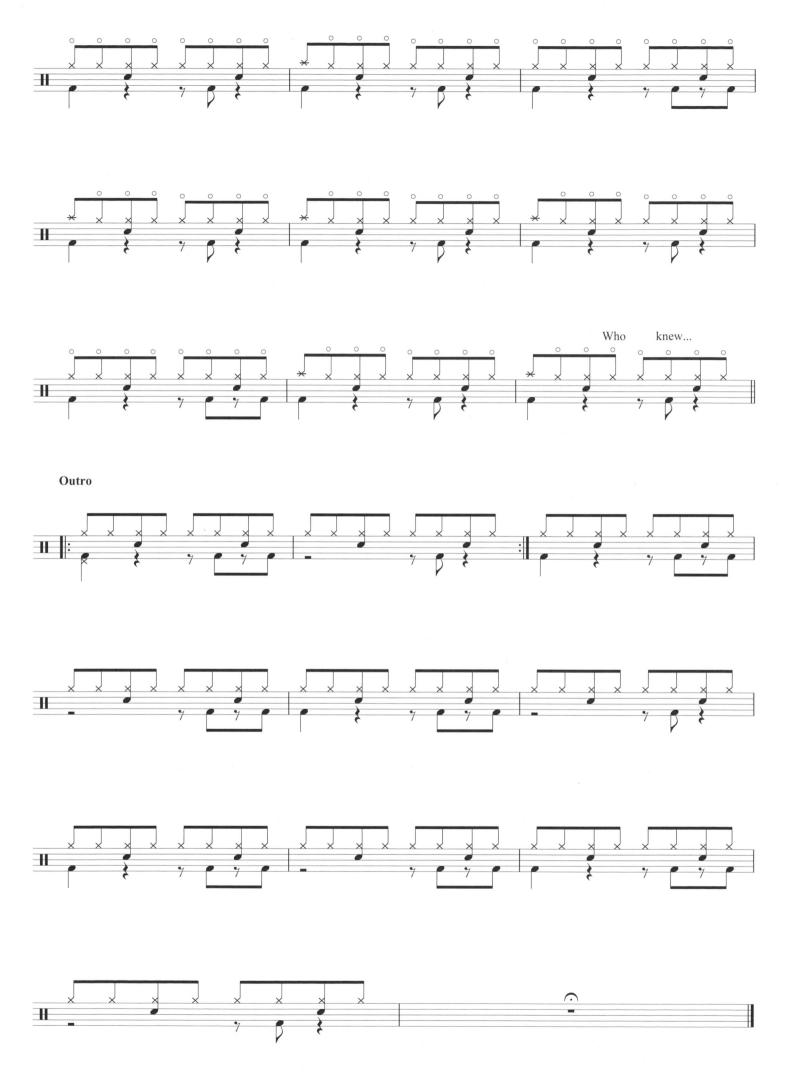

155

Y.M.C.A.

Words and Music by Jacques Morali, Henri Belolo and Victor Willis

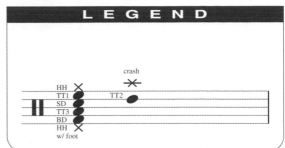

Intro
Moderate Disco ♩ = 126

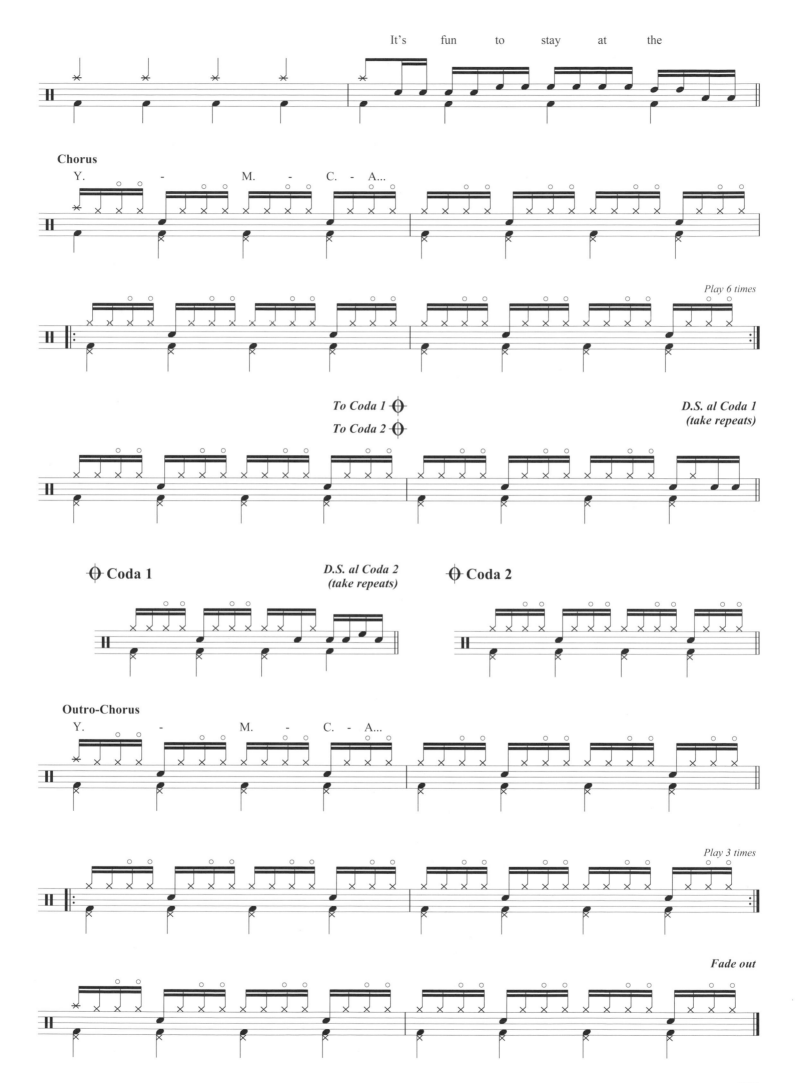

It's fun to stay at the

Chorus
Y. - M. - C. - A...

Play 6 times

To Coda 1 ⊕
To Coda 2 ⊕

D.S. al Coda 1
(take repeats)

⊕ **Coda 1**

D.S. al Coda 2
(take repeats)

⊕ **Coda 2**

Outro-Chorus
Y. - M. - C. - A...

Play 3 times

Fade out

You Belong With Me

Words and Music by Taylor Swift and Liz Rose

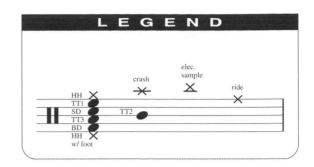

Intro
Moderately ♩ = 130

Verse
You're   on   the phone...

1., 3.   2.   4.

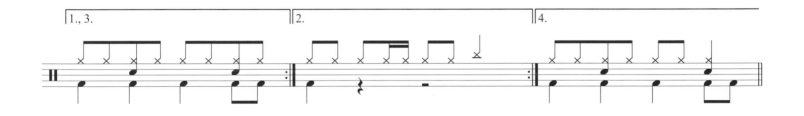

Pre-Chorus
She   wears   short   skirts...

Chorus

If you could see...

*Play ride on edge throughout.

sim.

You be - long with me...

Verse

Walk in the streets...

1.

2.

159

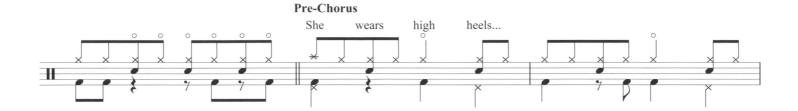

Pre-Chorus

She wears high heels...

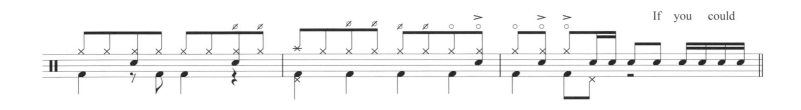

If you could

Chorus

see...

sim.

Guitar Solo

Bridge

...driv - in' to my house...

Can't you

Chorus

see...

me...

You Oughta Know

Lyrics by Alanis Morissette
Music by Alanis Morissette and Glen Ballard

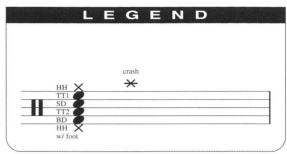

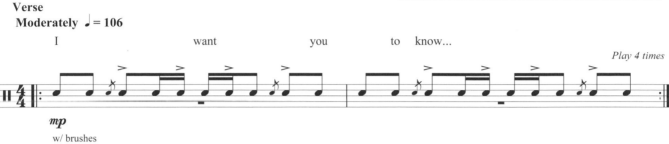

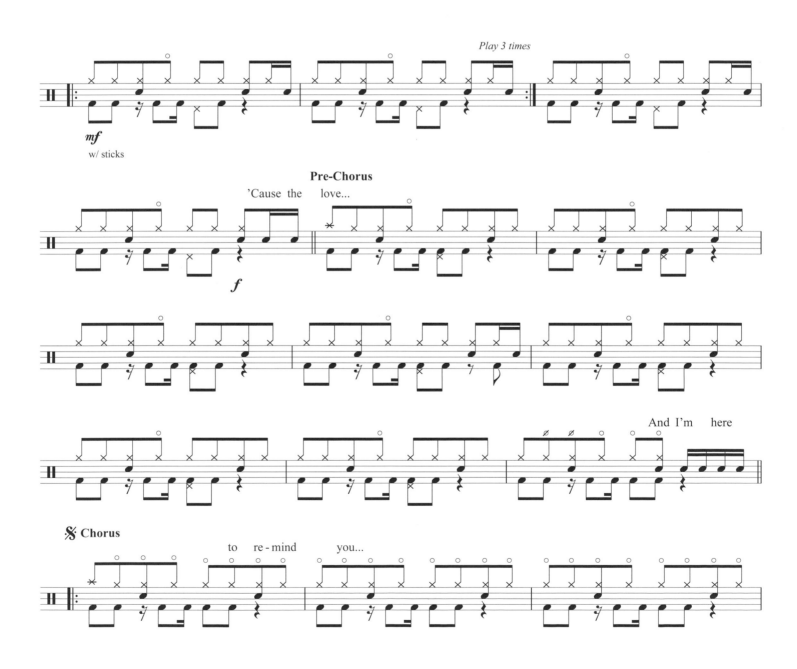

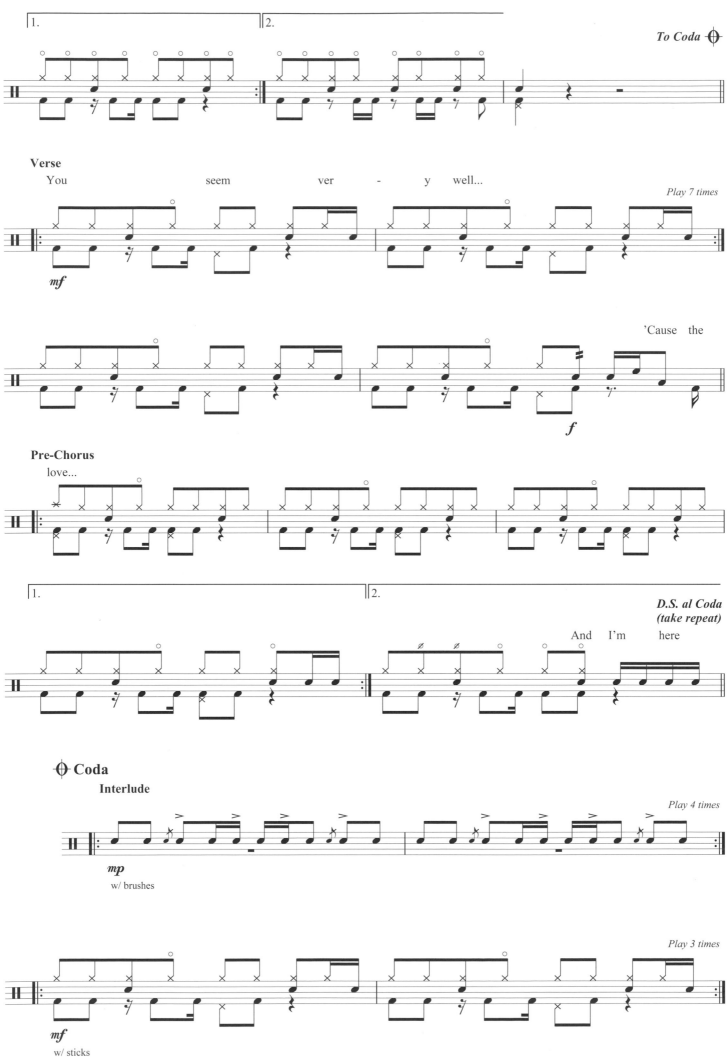

Verse

You seem ver - y well...

Play 7 times

'Cause the

Pre-Chorus

love...

1.   **2.**

D.S. al Coda
(take repeat)

And I'm here

Coda

Interlude

Play 4 times

mp
w/ brushes

Play 3 times

mf
w/ sticks

YOU CAN'T BEAT OUR DRUM BOOKS!

Bass Drum Control
Best Seller for More Than 50 Years!
by Colin Bailey
This perennial favorite among drummers helps players develop their bass drum technique and increase their flexibility through the mastery of exercises.
06620020 Book/Online Audio $17.99

The Complete Drumset Rudiments
by Peter Magadini
Use your imagination to incorporate these rudimental etudes into new patterns that you can apply to the drumset or tom toms as you develop your hand technique with the Snare Drum Rudiments, your hand and foot technique with the Drumset Rudiments and your polyrhythmic technique with the Polyrhythm Rudiments. Adopt them all into your own creative expressions based on ideas you come up with while practicing.
06620016 Book/CD Pack $14.95

Drum Aerobics
by Andy Ziker
A 52-week, one-exercise-per-day workout program for developing, improving, and maintaining drum technique. Players of all levels – beginners to advanced – will increase their speed, coordination, dexterity and accuracy. The online audio contains all 365 workout licks, plus play-along grooves in styles including rock, blues, jazz, heavy metal, reggae, funk, calypso, bossa nova, march, mambo, New Orleans 2nd Line, and lots more!
06620137 Book/Online Audio $19.99

Drumming the Easy Way!
The Beginner's Guide to Playing Drums for Students and Teachers
by Tom Hapke
Cherry Lane Music
Now with online audio! This book takes the beginning drummer through the paces – from reading simple exercises to playing great grooves and fills. Each lesson includes a preparatory exercise and a solo. Concepts and rhythms are introduced one at a time, so growth is natural and easy. Features large, clear musical print, intensive treatment of each individual drum figure, solos following each exercise to motivate students, and more!
02500876 Book/Online Audio.................................$19.99
02500191 Book...$14.99

The Drumset Musician – 2nd Edition
by Rod Morgenstein and Rick Mattingly
Containing hundreds of practical, usable beats and fills, *The Drumset Musician* teaches you how to apply a variety of patterns and grooves to the actual performance of songs. The accompanying online audio includes demos as well as 18 play-along tracks covering a wide range of rock, blues and pop styles, with detailed instructions on how to create exciting, solid drum parts.
00268369 Book/Online Audio..............................$19.99

Instant Guide to Drum Grooves
The Essential Reference for the Working Drummer
by Maria Martinez
Become a more versatile drumset player! From traditional Dixieland to cutting-edge hip-hop, *Instant Guide to Drum Grooves* is a handy source featuring 100 patterns that will prepare working drummers for the stylistic variety of modern gigs. The book includes essential beats and grooves in such styles as: jazz, shuffle, country, rock, funk, New Orleans, reggae, calypso, Brazilian and Latin.
06620056 Book/CD Pack $12.99

1001 Drum Grooves
The Complete Resource for Every Drummer
by Steve Mansfield
Cherry Lane Music
This book presents 1,001 drumset beats played in a variety of musical styles, past and present. It's ideal for beginners seeking a well-organized, easy-to-follow encyclopedia of drum grooves, as well as consummate professionals who want to bring their knowledge of various drum styles to new heights. Author Steve Mansfield presents: rock and funk grooves, blues and jazz grooves, ethnic grooves, Afro-Cuban and Caribbean grooves, and much more.
02500337 Book..$14.99

Polyrhythms – The Musician's Guide
by Peter Magadini
edited by Wanda Sykes
Peter Magadini's *Polyrhythms* is acclaimed the world over and has been hailed by *Modern Drummer* magazine as "by far the best book on the subject." Written for instrumentalists and vocalists alike, this book with online audio contains excellent solos and exercises that feature polyrhythmic concepts. Topics covered include: 6 over 4, 5 over 4, 7 over 4, 3 over 4, 11 over 4, and other rhythmic ratios; combining various polyrhythms; polyrhythmic time signatures; and much more. The audio includes demos of the exercises and is accessed online using the unique code in each book.
06620053 Book/Online Audio..$19.99

Joe Porcaro's Drumset Method – Groovin' with Rudiments
Patterns Applied to Rock, Jazz & Latin Drumset
by Joe Porcaro
Master teacher Joe Porcaro presents rudiments at the drumset in this sensational new edition of *Groovin' with Rudiments*. This book is chock full of exciting drum grooves, sticking patterns, fills, polyrhythmic adaptations, odd meters, and fantastic solo ideas in jazz, rock, and Latin feels. The online audio features 99 audio clip examples in many styles to round out this true collection of superb drumming material for every serious drumset performer.
06620129 Book/Online Audio $24.99

66 Drum Solos for the Modern Drummer
Rock • Funk • Blues • Fusion • Jazz
by Tom Hapke
Cherry Lane Music
66 Drum Solos for the Modern Drummer presents drum solos in all styles of music in an easy-to-read format. These solos are designed to help improve your technique, independence, improvisational skills, and reading ability on the drums and at the same time provide you with some cool licks that you can use right away in your own playing.
02500319 Book/Online Audio..$17.99

HAL•LEONARD®
www.halleonard.com